The Texts of Shakespeare

Related titles

The Arden Handbook of Shakespeare and Early Modern Drama
Edited by Michelle M. Dowd and Tom Rutter

The Arden Introduction to Reading Shakespeare: Close Reading and Analysis
Jeremy Lopez

Essential Shakespeare: The Arden Guide to Text and Interpretation (Second Edition)
Pamela Bickley and Jenny Stevens

Shakespearean Tragedy
Kiernan Ryan

Shakespeare's First Folio 1623–2023: Text and Afterlives
Edited by Matthias Bauer and Angelika Zirker

The Texts of Shakespeare

The Transformation of Popular Theatre to Printed Book

Stephen Orgel

THE ARDEN SHAKESPEARE
LONDON · NEW YORK · OXFORD · NEW DELHI · SYDNEY

THE ARDEN SHAKESPEARE

Bloomsbury Publishing Plc, 50 Bedford Square, London, WC1B 3DP, UK
Bloomsbury Publishing Inc. 1359 Broadway, 12th Floor New York, NY 10018 USA
Bloomsbury Publishing Ireland, 29 Earlsfort Terrace, Dublin 2, D02 AY28, Ireland

BLOOMSBURY, THE ARDEN SHAKESPEARE and the Arden Shakespeare logo
are trademarks of Bloomsbury Publishing Plc

First published in Great Britain 2026

Copyright © Stephen Orgel, 2026

Stephen Orgel has asserted his right under the Copyright, Designs and
Patents Act, 1988, to be identified as author of this work.

Cover design: Ben Anslow
Cover images © AdobeStock

All rights reserved. No part of this publication may be: i) reproduced or
transmitted in any form, electronic or mechanical, including photocopying,
recording or by means of any information storage or retrieval system without
prior permission in writing from the publishers; or ii) used or reproduced in
any way for the training, development or operation of artificial intelligence (AI)
technologies, including generative AI technologies. The rights holders expressly
reserve this publication from the text and data mining exception as per
Article 4(3) of the Digital Single Market Directive (EU) 2019/790.

Bloomsbury Publishing Plc does not have any control over, or responsibility for,
any third-party websites referred to or in this book. All internet addresses given
in this book were correct at the time of going to press. The author and publisher
regret any inconvenience caused if addresses have changed or sites have
ceased to exist, but can accept no responsibility for any such changes.

A catalogue record for this book is available from the British Library.

A catalog record for this book is available from the Library of Congress.

ISBN: HB: 978-1-3505-6105-2
       PB: 978-1-3505-6104-5
       ePDF: 978-1-3505-6106-9
       eBook: 978-1-3505-6107-6

Typeset by RefineCatch Limited, Bungay, Suffolk

For product safety related questions contact productsafety@bloomsbury.com.

To find out more about our authors and books visit www.bloomsbury.com
and sign up for our newsletters.

For Richard Corum and Constance Filbin

Contents

Preface viii

1. The Texts of Shakespeare 1
2. The Poems 17
3. Romeo and Juliet 37
4. Hamlet 57
5. King Lear 71
6. Pericles Prince of Tyre 93
7. Macbeth 101
8. The Folio 115

Conclusion 131

Notes 153
Bibliography 167
Index 175

Preface

My book *The Globe in Print* (Oxford: Oxford University Press, 2024) discussed the transformation of plays to books in the sixteenth and early seventeenth centuries, the great age of early English theatre, and my *The Idea of the Book and the Creation of Literature* (Oxford: Oxford University Press, 2023) took a longer view of the transformation of performance of all kinds into books. *The Texts of Shakespeare* considers what is for us inevitably the crucial instance, and the three books necessarily cover some of the same ground. There are many excellent recent works on Shakespeare's texts—by David Kastan, Laurie Maguire, Andrew Gurr, Emma Smith, Ben Higgins, Tiffany Stern, Zachary Lesser, to single out only a small number—but these tend to address specialists, readers who are already expert in the field of textual studies. The present volume assumes a much more general readership. It is based on my teaching decades of introductory Shakespeare courses, at Harvard, Berkeley, Johns Hopkins, and finally for thirty-two years at Stanford. It is also based on a number of specialized essays of my own, collected in *The Authentic Shakespeare* (New York: Routledge, 2002), *Imagining Shakespeare* (Houndmills: Palgrave Macmillan, 2003), *Spectacular Performances* (Manchester: Manchester University Press, 2011), and *The Invention of Shakespeare* (Philadelphia: University of Pennsylvania Press, 2022).

I am happy to acknowledge many years of discussions with the late Anne Barton, Marion Trousdale, Paul Alpers, David Kalstone, Jonas Barish, and the greatest teacher I ever had, Andrew Chiappe, dear friends and superb guides, now all sadly gone. David Kastan's *Shakespeare and the Book* (Cambridge: Cambridge University Press, 2001) and Tiffany Stern's *Documents of Performance in Early Modern England* (Cambridge: Cambridge University Press, 2009) have been essential resources throughout. Tiffany Stern and Tom Bishop have been most generous with their expertise, and the work and friendship of David Kastan and Peter Stallybrass have been a constant inspiration.

I have benefitted greatly from decades of superb students, of whom I can here name only a few: at Harvard Stephen Weissman and Rebecca Hoge Shankland; at Berkeley Joseph Westlund, Allan Paulson, Robert Fulton and Richard Corum; at Johns Hopkins Mark Crispin Miller, Katharine Eisaman Maus, Lindsay Kaplan, Laura Levine and Jane Tylus; at Stanford Bradin Cormack, Michael Wyatt, Richard Preiss, James Marino, Carolyn Sale, David Goldstein and Deanne Williams. The dedication to Richard Corum, author of an exemplary guide to teaching *Hamlet*, and his wife the artist Connie Filbin, records in addition a deep and fruitful friendship of over sixty years.

A note on the modern Shakespeare quotations

The modern Shakespeare quotations cited throughout are from *The Complete Pelican Shakespeare*, General Editors Stephen Orgel and A. R. Braunmuller. London: Penguin Classics, 2002.

1

The Texts of Shakespeare

To begin with, Shakespeare plays were not books. They were scripts designed to eventuate in performance. The term 'script' for the text of a play apparently dates only from the nineteenth century; it also implies that the work is written by hand. In Shakespeare's time what we call the script was called 'the book of the play'. 'The book of the play' was not the play, but only a part of it, a manuscript of the dialogue, with minimal instructions for performance. A text in the early modern period did not need to be printed to be a book (and even today, the 'book' of a musical is not the musical, but only its text; this 'book' is rarely if ever published). Moreover, the plot of the play was different from the play itself, and was written before the dialogue and circulated separately; and thus the dialogue of a play could be the work of several authors, none of whom was the author of the plot. As Tiffany Stern observes, 'Plotting was ... a separate skill from play-writing, because plots themselves were different documents from plays'.[1] Hence plays were often thought of as patchworks, amalgams of a number of discrete documents, and playwrights were derisively called play-patchers.

The play itself was the work as realized on stage, in action, costume and spectacle—an amalgam of still more elements—and by the time the work got to the stage, even with a single author of the dialogue, it was profoundly collaborative. (There are, to be sure, purely literary plays, like *Samson Agonistes*, but they took their form from stage plays.) To turn the play then into a published book required still more collaboration, in the form of a good deal of editorial intervention. Plays were sometimes commissioned by a theatrical company to capitalize on some currently notorious event, in which the company, not the playwright or the 'plot-wright', was properly the 'inventor'.[2] The plot of James Shirley's *The Gamester* was provided by King Charles himself, and the play was devised to be performed before the king; in this case, the audience was the inventor.[3]

The script of the play belonged to the company, and in the course of staging, it would be revised as they saw fit—the company owned the play. The term playwright was originally a degrading one, the maker of plays conceived not as a poet but as a craftsman, on the model of 'wheelwright' or 'cartwright'. Most playwrights were what we would call free-lancers, though some signed contracts requiring them to write for only one company. Playwrights for the popular theatre were typically employees, and wrote what they were commissioned to write—they were given the plot, often with the scenes parcelled out among several playwrights. The sort of control that modern playwrights like Arthur Miller or Tennessee Williams were able to exercise over the production and reproduction of their work was unknown in the early modern period. (Shakespeare was an exception: as a part-owner of the company he wrote for and performed in, he was literally his own boss.) The only readers assumed by the first play-texts were initially the managers of the company and then the individual actors—who, however, had only their own parts with their cue lines, not the whole play. The complete text was the copy that was submitted to the Master of the Revels, who censored whatever he deemed dangerous or impolitic and provided the necessary licence allowing the play to be performed, with the stipulation, as revealing as it was unenforceable, that no more be spoken than was in the text. This copy either was the basis of or directly became the prompt-book. (Official censorship of the stage was in force in Britain until 1968.) It was in the company's interest to have as few copies of the complete play in existence as possible, to preclude it falling into the hands of a rival company or of a printer.

The first Shakespeare plays to appear in print were *The Taming of the Shrew*, *Titus Andronicus* and the play now called 2 *Henry VI*, but in its first iteration called *The First part of the Contention betwixt the two Famous Houses of Yorke and Lancaster, with the death of the good Duke Humphrey*. These all were published in 1594, by which time Shakespeare had been writing plays for the London stage for at least four years. None of the published versions included Shakespeare's name. In the previous year, however, the long poem *Venus and Adonis* was published; this had a dedication to the young Earl of Southampton, which was signed by Shakespeare (Shakespeare's name is not on the title page); and in 1594 another long poem appeared, *The Rape of Lucrece*, also dedicated to Southampton and signed by Shakespeare.

Shakespeare's turn to narrative poetry has been explained by the fact that the London theatres were closed in 1593 because of plague, and therefore the actors and playwrights were out of work, but this does not account for the kind of poetry Shakespeare wrote. The turn from drama to narrative poetry seems natural enough, except that these poems, stanzaic and formal, look so little like the plays. *Lucrece*, moreover, a story of sexual violence, includes a great deal of pictorial description that loses sight of the narrative.

Shakespeare's name first appears on the title page of a book in 1598. In that year *Love's Labour's Lost*, a second and third edition of *Richard II* and a second edition of *Richard III* name the author as William Shake-speare or W. Shakespere—Shakespeare's name, variously spelled, had become a selling point. In 1600 it appeared on the title page of *The Most Excellent Historie of the Merchant of Venice* ('Written by William Shakespeare') and *A Midsommernights dreame*, but not on the title page of 3 *Henry VI* (under the title *The True Tragedie of Richard Duke of Yorke, and the death of good King Henrie the Sixt*). The title page of the first quarto of *Hamlet*, 1603, reads *The Tragicall Historie of Hamlet Prince of Denmarke. By William Shake-speare*. On the title page of the second quarto, in the next year, he is *William Shakespeare*.

A word about bibliographic terminology: plays were typically published throughout the early modern era in small formats, quartos or octavos—the largest standard book size was the folio (the word means 'leaf') for which the printing sheet consisted of two double-sided leaves, four pages, and the sheet was folded in half. Folios were large, expensive books and were the format for serious and important works, typically philosophy, history, science, classics—publishing a collection of modern plays in folio constituted a considerable rise in dignity for popular drama. To produce a quarto (a 'fourth') the printing sheet was folded again crosswise, producing four double-sided leaves, eight pages. Quartos in Shakespeare's age typically sold for sixpence, a day's wages for a skilled workman, so those people, even if they were literate, did not buy many quartos. For an octavo ('eighth') the sheet was folded again to make eight leaves and sixteen pages. Play quartos and octavos were typically sold unbound, merely stitched together with string, and most have not survived—Shakespeare quartos are now far rarer than Shakespeare folios, though they were produced in larger numbers. But to put the matter of Shakespeare's currency with readers in perspective, the most popular Shakespeare play quartos went through between four and eight editions over a period of two or three decades, whereas Sir Thomas Overbury's long moralizing poem *The Wife* went through five editions *in the first year of its publication alone*, 1614, and in ten editions before 1618.

In the sixteenth century it was typically the name of the acting company, with its aristocratic patron, or the fact that the play was performed at court, that was assumed to attract buyers. But by 1600 Shakespeare was popular enough that his name was assumed to make a book marketable, and it therefore also appears on a number of works by other less well known writers. Moreover, press censorship in Elizabethan and Jacobean England was far less rigid than censorship of the stage. In contrast to censorship of theatre, Cyndia Clegg observes that 'government enactments affecting printing, as well as practices in the printing trade, are often contradictory and idiosyncratic: the fabric of Elizabethan press censorship and control is a crazy quilt of proclamations, patents, trade regulations, judicial decrees, and privy council and parliamentary actions patched together by the sometimes common and sometimes competing threads of religious, economic, political, and private interests'.[4] But theatre involved crowds and raised passions, and was therefore considered far more dangerous than books.

Here is a very clear indication of the difference between the regulation of performance and of books. In 1610 a troupe of players in Yorkshire were arrested and charged with sedition. Their offense was performing *Pericles*, *King Lear*, and a lost play about Saint George that the authorities claimed were (or perhaps had had introduced into them) Roman Catholic propaganda—the members of the troupe were Catholic. The actors testified, however, that their performing texts of *Pericles* and *King Lear* were the published quartos. These had been duly licensed for publication and therefore could not be considered seditious. But this was not considered an adequate defence: the licensing of books is a different matter from the licensing of play scripts. Public performances are much more dangerous than individual readers or family groups. In 1610 the published play was not equivalent to the play in performance.

Even famous plays, and those that had been rewritten for publication, were often published anonymously. *Tamburlaine* was not definitely ascribed to Marlowe until the nineteenth century; Kyd was first named as the author of *The Spanish Tragedy* (a famous play several times updated, and performed continuously since the 1580s) in Thomas Heywood's *Apology for Actors* in 1612. Nevertheless, in being credited with the published versions of his plays, Shakespeare was exceptional but not unique. Well before Shakespeare, in 1565, Thomas Sackville and Thomas Norton, two aristocratic lawyers, are named as the authors of *Gorboduc* on its first publication, and again when it was reissued under the title *The Tragidie of Ferrex and Porrex* in 1570. The Cambridge academic Thomas Preston, author of the famous and popular *Cambises*, is identified on the title pages of editions in 1570 and 1595; Christopher Marlowe and Thomas Nashe are named as the authors of *Dido Queene of Carthage* on its first publication in 1594, and both *The Massacre at Paris* and *Edward II* are credited to Marlowe on their title pages in 1594. When *Edward II* was reissued in 1598 it also bore Marlowe's name. John Lyly's *The Woman in the Moone* in 1597 bears his name. In the early 1600s John Marston's plays are attributed to him on their title pages (though when they were reissued in 1633, by which time he had been in holy orders for almost two decades, he protested and his name was removed). And literary plays—what has come to be called Closet Drama, plays designed for reading or private performance—were generally issued with an author's name: thus the title page of *Antonie* in 1595, a translation from the French of the famous sixteenth-century poet and dramatist Robert Garnier, declares that it was 'Doone into English by the Countess of Pembroke'. Samuel Daniel was named as the author of *Cleopatra* on its publication in 1594, 1595, and 1598.

Turning plays into books was a complicated matter, and involved a number of transformations. A spectator's account of the first performance of *Gorboduc* makes clear that the published text of the play, which is what survives, was very different from what was performed before the queen.[5] Both *Tamburlaine* and *The Spanish Tragedy* acknowledge that they have been rewritten for publication, and from about 1600 printed plays often advertise that they include more than the performing text. Ben Jonson repeatedly declared that his true audience was readers, and blamed the actors for the failure of his plays *Catiline* and *The New Inn*. Humphrey Moseley, issuing the works of Beaumont and Fletcher, is explicit about the difference between the play as a script and the play as a book:

> When these *Comedies* and *Tragedies* were presented on the Stage, the *Actours* omitted some *Scenes* and Passages (with the *Authour's* consent) as occasion led them; . . . But now you have both All that was *Acted*, and all that was not; even the perfect full Originalls without the least mutilation; So that were the *Authours* living . . . they themselves would challenge neither more nor lesse then what is here published . . . .[6]

For Moseley, performance mutilates the play; it is the book that preserves 'the perfect full originals'.

Moseley thus implies that he is printing the texts the playwrights gave to the actors, which were then revised for performance. This, of course, cannot be the case: turning scripts into books requires a good deal of editorial intervention, and there is no way of knowing what the texts were like that Moseley started with. Ben Jonson acknowledges that he has rewritten his plays for publication, and there is a good deal in Jonson's drama that is addressed solely to readers—prefatory essays, character sketches in the *dramatis personae*, marginal commentary, and especially the introductory epigrams to *Volpone* and *The Alchemist*, which include the plays' titles as acrostics, impossible to convey in anything but a printed text.

The first reference to Shakespeare as a playwright is a hostile allusion in the cautionary romance *Greene's Groatsworth of Wit* (1592), said to be the last work written by Robert Greene, but probably by somebody else whose identity is uncertain (the leading candidates are the writer and printer Henry Chettle and Greene's friend the satirist Thomas Nashe). A well-educated gentleman reduced by poverty to writing plays warns other playwrights,

> there is an upstart Crow, beautified with our feathers, that with his *Tygers hart wrapt in a Players hyde,* supposes he is as able to

bombast out a blanke verse as the best of you: and beeing an absolute *Johannes fac totum* [Jack of all trades], is in his owne conceit the onely Shake-scene in a countrey.

(fol. F1v)

The 'upstart crow' is Shakespeare, the country boy who never attended university, who nevertheless competes with highly educated playwrights like Greene and Christopher Marlowe. 'Beautified with our feathers' may imply an additional charge of plagiarism, or simply that his plays imitate ours. The passage identifies Shakespeare as both playwright and performer (a 'player' is an actor). 'Tygers hart wrapt in a Players hyde' parodies the line 'O tiger's heart wrapped in a woman's hide' from Shakespeare's early history play now known as *3 Henry VI* (1.4.137 in modern editions), preserved in the first folio as *The Third Part of Henry the Sixt with the death of the Duke of Yorke*, but known in its earliest published version as *The True Tragedie of Richard Duke of Yorke, and the death of good King Henrie the Sixt, with the Whole Contention betweene the two Houses Lancaster and Yorke*—there is no way of knowing what the play was called on the stage, before it became a book.[7] This alone is an indication of the transformations plays underwent when they became books, and how new editions involved further transformations. But what is especially striking is that the allusion was to a play not yet in print, which suggests a large theatre audience with good memories who were also readers of satirical pamphlets.

By the time *King Lear* was published in 1608, Shakespeare's name was famous enough to be in the largest type and come first on the title page. The text, however, as we shall see, has undergone very little editorial intervention; there are passages that frankly make no sense, and others where the printers have clearly misunderstood their copy. The text appears to be some version of Shakespeare's original draft; his handwriting was difficult, and his spelling eccentric and erratic. This would have been the copy that was delivered to the acting company before any performing changes; the clear text that was sent to the censor for approval would obviously not have been sent to the printer, but would have been kept by the company. By 1608, then, there was a reading public for Shakespeare plays; but judging from the shorter text that was eventually included in the folios, which appears at least in part to have been cut for performance, the text of the quarto was quite different from what one could hear in the theatre.

Eighteen of Shakespeare's thirty-seven plays were published in quarto editions before the collected edition of the first folio in 1623, which means that if there had been no folio, about half of Shakespeare's plays would be lost to us—there would be no *As You Like It, Twelfth Night, Macbeth, Anthony and Cleopatra, The Tempest, The Winter's Tale*. Without exception, the texts of the quartos are very different from the texts of the folio, often (though not always) significantly shorter, and with texts that are very different from those that have become standard for us. Many of the quartos seem to be, unlike the *King Lear* quarto, cut for performance; several seem to derive from actors' parts, others from the reports of spectators, which, in comparison with the texts that have become standard, seem very approximate (a striking example is the 1600 quarto of *Henry V*, which differs from the folio text not only in language but in significant elements of the plot). The editors of the first folio, Shakespeare's fellow-actors John Heminges and Henry Condell, dismiss the quartos as 'stolne and surreptitious', and declare the texts in the folio 'the true and perfect coppie', but it is clear that the texts of plays underwent changes as the venue and the audience changed—the play before the king was not the play at the Globe; the version at the popular Globe was different from the play at the elite Blackfriars theatre. And plays at court were typically much longer than plays in the public playhouses; so revisions, additions, and cuts would have been constant and commonplace. The opening chorus of *Romeo and Juliet* famously alludes to 'the two-hours' traffic of our stage'. Two hours is an impossibly short performing time for all but a very few plays of the period, but Tiffany Stern, in a fascinating article on systems of time-measurement in the early modern period, argues that 'two hours' is not to be taken literally, and cites instances of plays being said to take three hours, or even more.[8] The measurement of time was, moreover, very approximate; and the two hour reference in *Romeo and Juliet* may only be saying how the time will seem to fly.

The text changed constantly. There are three versions of *Hamlet* and *Romeo and Juliet*, two of *King Lear*, and of every other play that exists in both quarto and folio versions, which often differ markedly from each other. These are not the only versions of the plays that existed, however; they are only what has survived because they were printed. But every performance is different from every other performance, and for every revival the text would have been reconsidered and revised. In fact, we have some hard evidence on the subject: for two plays by George Peele, *Alcazar* and *Orlando*, we have, for *Alcazar*, the stage manager's summary of the action, and for *Orlando*, the actor Edward Alleyn's acting part, the performing script for his role. But the published quartos of both these plays differ markedly from the evidence of what actually went on onstage. Indeed, there was no assumption in the period that the text was established or final. Milton's copy of the Shakespeare folio has recently been identified. It is full of annotations; some of these are corrections, but most are alternative readings—places where the folio makes perfectly good sense, but Milton marginally provides a version he finds preferable. Sometimes the change derives from a quarto, but sometimes it is simply Milton improving the play.[9]

In short, the text of drama was both unstable and deeply collaborative. The playwright (or playwrights: many plays had multiple authors) was typically paid by the company to supply a manuscript, which then was the property of the company, and the company revised it as they saw fit. But the play did not constitute what we would call intellectual property, which was not yet a category in law, and the playwright (or indeed, anyone with a manuscript, including the acting company) could also sell it to a publisher. Actors might undertake to compose a complete version of the play out of their individual parts, supplying what they remembered of the other roles, and sell that. In so far as any notion of copyright existed, it belonged to the publisher—there were no royalties, and any profit from the sale of the work belonged to the publisher, who had bought the manuscript outright and now owned it, just as the acting company owned their manuscript of the play and were free to sell it.

Thomas Heywood, in a preface to his play *The Rape of Lucrece* (1608), explains his unwillingness to publish his plays:

> some have used a double sale of their labours, first to the Stage and after to the Presse: For my owne part, I here proclaim my selfe ever faithfull in the first, and never guilty of the last: yet since some of my Playes have (unknowne to me, and without any of my direction) accidentally come into the Printers hands, and therefore so corrupt and mangled, (copied onely by the eare) that I have been unable to know them, as ashamed to challenge them. This therefore I was the willinger to furnish out in his native habit....[10]

It has been doubted that there was any shorthand system at the time capable of recording a play, but Heywood's testimony is surely sufficient—sufficient also to indicate how inexact the transcription inevitably was. There were, in fact, ten systems of shorthand published in England between 1588 and 1626, and Tiffany Stern has provided ample evidence of audiences taking notes at theatre, moreover not necessarily in shorthand.[11] Clearly there was a readers' market for plays, even corrupt and mangled ones; and soon enough plays were being treated as literary property.

The 'bad' first quarto of *Hamlet* (1603) includes passages that are marked with marginal double quotes. Zachary Lesser and Peter Stallybrass interpret these as commonplacing marks; the marginal quotes identify the passages as excerptible bits of wisdom appropriate to be copied out into one's commonplace book. Tiffany Stern's analysis of the volume suggests instead that the printed text was composed of written reports by several different auditors at different times, and the double quotes indicated passages that were in some reports but not in others, and therefore were sometimes omitted. The printed text was thus an anthology of what one heard at various performances.[12] (Marginal double quotes were used in both ways in the seventeenth century.) In the first case, the play is being treated as literature; in the second, the play in the book was significantly different from the play in the theatre.

Here are some other perplexing examples: when Cassio is first mentioned in *Othello*, he is described as 'a fellow almost damned in a fair wife', but the wife is never mentioned again, and for the remainder of the play Cassio is clearly unmarried. Early in *The Tempest*, Ferdinand alludes to a son of Antonio's among those lost in the wreck, but thereafter Antonio has no son. In *The Comedy of Errors*, a servant named Luce appears at the beginning of Act 3; in the next scene she is named Nell. These are evidence, doubtless, that Shakespeare sometimes changed his mind during the process of composition, the most puzzling aspect of which is why they remained a permanent feature of the texts: did the actors playing Cassio and Antonio not wonder about the missing wife and son? Did the boy cast as Luce/Nell not demand to know, as soon as he got his part, what his name was? How did the confusion survive the first rehearsal? And of course, we do not know that they did—what was the relation between the texts that were published and what was given to the actors and spoken on stage?

In 1619 the publisher and printer William Jaggard, in association with the publisher Thomas Pavier, began reprinting Shakespeare quartos, including quartos of two plays not by Shakespeare but that had been ascribed to him: *A Woman Killed With Kindness* and *Sir John Oldcastle*. The latter was a play written to correct Shakespeare's version of Oldcastle in the character of Falstaff, which nevertheless in Jaggard's edition has Shakespeare's name on the title page (followed, however, by a note affirming that the play is not by Shakespeare).[13] As providing material for a collected Shakespeare, this has been viewed as an attempt to pre-empt the project that became the first folio. It may not have been as focused as this suggests, but it was certainly surreptitious, since Jaggard did not own the rights to several of the plays, and the project was halted when the King's Men protested, though Jaggard continued to publish pirated quartos with false dates on their title pages.[14] There were clearly no hard feelings, however, since Jaggard was also the printer of the folio.

The folio, with its claim to enshrine 'the true and perfect coppie' of every play, undertook to establish a correct text of Shakespearean drama. This lasted, however, only until the publication of the second folio in 1632, which, though it looks like a page for page reprint of the first, in fact corrects a number of what its editors take to be errors. (Some of these are dubious: for example, in *Love's Labour's Lost* it corrects mistakes in the pedant Holofernes's Latin; but are these really errors in the text, or is the point that Holofernes's Latin is at fault?) And the second issue of the third folio, followed by the fourth (1664 and 1685), adds seven plays to the thirty-six in the original collection (of which only *Pericles* is still part of the canon). The next edition, of Nicholas Rowe, in 1709 made further corrections and modernized the text. It was also the first collected Shakespeare to include the poems, in an additional volume issued in 1710. Over the next centuries new editions appeared at regular intervals, all claiming to provide a correct and therefore stable text, but all differing from each other to some degree. And since the texts were almost invariably modernized, they moved increasingly away from the Shakespeare of the folios and quartos, and of course even farther away from the experience of Shakespeare's stage.

There were, then, many different versions of the text of any play, and there was nothing fixed about the script—or ultimately about the text.

All those versions of *Romeo and Juliet* are *Romeo and Juliet*—the three surviving from Shakespeare's era, and the multitude of rewritings over the centuries: there was no final or correct version of the play. Here is an example, from the most famous speech in the play, Juliet's balcony soliloquy beginning 'O Romeo, Romeo, wherefore art thou Romeo?' Since the eighteenth century, the standard modern text has read,

> What's Montague? It is nor hand, nor foot,
> Nor arm, nor face, nor any other part
> Belonging to a man. O be some other name!
> What's in a name? That which we call a rose
> By any other name would smell as sweet.
>
> (2.2.40–44)

Editors have three early texts of this play to work from. The first quarto (1597) reads this way:

> Whats *Mountague?* It is nor hand nor foote,
> Nor arme, nor face, nor any other part.
> Whats in a name? That which we call a Rose,
> By any other name would smell as sweet . . . .

Here is passage in the second quarto (1599):

> Whats *Mountague?* It is nor hand nor foote,
> Nor arme, nor face, ô be some other name
> Belonging to a man.
> Whats in a name that which we call a rose,
> By any other name would smell as sweete . . . .

And here is the first folio (1623):

> Whats *Mountague?* It is nor hand nor foote,
> Nor arme, nor face, O be some other name
> Belonging to a man.
> What? in a names that which we call a Rose,
> By any other word would smell as sweete . . . .

There is, in fact, no early text that reads as our modern text does—and this is the most famous speech in the play. Instead, we have three different texts, all of which are clearly some version of the same speech, but none of which seems to us a final or satisfactory version. The beautiful passage in modern editions, the version that is universally performed now, is an editorial invention. Editors have conflated and revised the three versions into something we recognize as great poetry. Is this what Shakespeare 'really' wrote, or intended? Who can say?

The basis for all performances by Shakespeare's company was the prompt-book, but even that was not the play; it was just the version of the play that was revised and rethought whenever a new production was mounted. Or even a new performance: the play on the stage changed constantly. The play only became potentially stable when it became a book; but as the editorial history of Shakespeare makes clear, even printing the plays, even the monumental folios, and the multitude of subsequent editions, did not stabilize them: the text of every edition of Shakespeare is different from that of every other edition

For many years, starting in the eighteenth century, editors printed a conflation of the quarto and folio texts of *King Lear*, each of which includes material missing from the other. But that is clearly an editorial confection, and the preference now is to treat the two texts separately, but privilege the quarto, which is longer than the folio text, and therefore gives us more Shakespeare (thus implicitly declaring the folio deficient), but even more because it seems to derive from Shakespeare's holograph, and what editors generally want to see themselves as doing is getting back to what Shakespeare actually wrote, back before the book, to that thing that does not survive, Shakespeare's original manuscript.[15] This also means, paradoxically, that though Shakespeare's plays were written specifically for performance, the performing element is what we want to get rid of. What we want is a Shakespeare uncontaminated by the actors and the stage. But that is a complete fiction, something we have to invent—that Shakespeare exists only in the poems and sonnets, and even though *Venus and Adonis* and *Lucrece* are now far less well known and popular than the plays, increasingly for us those have become the models for Shakespeare the dramatist. Critics now sometimes insist that Shakespeare must have been writing for publication; but the first folio was not the publication. The critic's notional edition was the publication Shakespeare must proleptically have had in mind.

2

The Poems

For readers, in his own time Shakespeare was best known as the poet of *Venus and Adonis* and *The Rape of Lucrece*; and indeed, the popular dramatist's turn to poetry with these two long poems was clearly an attempt to fashion a different kind of career. None of the major English poetic figures of the late sixteenth century—Shakespeare, Marlowe, Sidney, Spenser, the young Donne—was a professional poet. Sidney was an aristocrat and independently wealthy; Shakespeare was an actor and part-owner of the theatrical company he performed in and wrote for; Marlowe was a number of things including playwright and spy; Spenser was a private secretary and then a civil servant in Ireland; Donne was a private secretary until he did himself out of a job by marrying his employer's ward without permission, and eventually had a very successful ecclesiastical career. Samuel Daniel and Michael Drayton look like professional poets to us, but Daniel was a tutor in a large aristocratic household for a long period, and Drayton, in addition to being a prolific poet, was a collaborative playwright and theatre manager.[1]

The major professional poets have for the most part disappeared from literary history: Thomas Churchyard, Thomas Tusser, George Turberville, George Gascoigne (Churchyard and Gascoigne started as professional soldiers). Poetry was, for the figures we consider the major poets, a means to some other end: for Sidney the end was social (in fact, biographers have a good deal of trouble dealing with Sidney's imaginative literature, treating it as merely something he did to fill his time while he was banished from court, though the disappointments and manipulativeness of *Astrophil and Stella* and the heroic aspirations, romance, and incipient tragedy of *Arcadia* are surely relevant to the world of court and politics). For Spenser poetry was a way of getting a better job, getting out of Ireland and installed at court, not necessarily as a poet—at this it failed: on the publication of the first three books of *The Faerie Queene*, Queen Elizabeth rewarded Spenser with the handsome sum of £100, but sent him back to Ireland. After this, he published regularly, but often with the aggrieved tone of *Colin Clout's Come Home Again*. For Marlowe... who knows? Writing was one of a number of things he did, perhaps simply as part of his education, perhaps to bring himself to the attention of important and powerful men who would be impressed with his wit and intelligence and dubious moral principles, and would employ him to do something other than write poetry.

Was his poetry, in fact, one of the things that attracted the attention of the statesman Burghley and the spy-master Walsingham? It showed that he was intelligent, well educated, and willing, and could adopt any number of alternative personae. It is also significant that for Donne, Marlowe, and for many years Spenser, nothing was published. (If Shakespeare had died, as Marlowe did, at the age of 29, he too would have published at most *Venus and Adonis*.) Manuscript circulation of poetry was an extension of the personal and social life, and a way of undertaking to control one's readership. Being known as a poet was also, for a gentleman, a step downward: as Donne wrote to his friend Sir Henry Goodyer in 1609, he sought for himself 'a graver course, then of a Poet, into which (that I may also keep my dignity) I would not seem to relapse'[2]—publication would be identifying himself as a professional writer, what we would call a hack.

For Shakespeare, one would say that writing narrative poems was a logical extension of writing plays, except that the poems look so little like the plays. This is less true of Marlowe; but Marlowe's *Hero and Leander*, and Shakespeare's *Venus and Adonis* and *The Rape of Lucrece* all have the look of attempts to craft a quite different kind of career from that of playwright. Marlowe's poem was unpublished at the time of his death, though it was licensed for publication four months later, so a manuscript was among his papers. It may also have been in circulation, though there is no evidence that this was the case—it is cited frequently after it was published in 1598, but except for the Stationers' Register entry in September, 1593, there is no early reference to it. It has been considered an influence on Shakespeare's Ovidian poem, though Marlowe's one reference to the Venus and Adonis legend—

> . . . Venus in her naked glory strove
> To please the careless and disdainful eyes
> Of proud Adonis, that before her lies[3]—

looks like an allusion to Shakespeare's version of the story, not to Ovid's. Was Shakespeare's poem circulating in manuscript before it was published?

Shakespeare's first two narrative poems appeared from the outset, so far as we know, as beautiful, carefully printed little books. When *Venus and Adonis* was published, the poet was not yet thirty. Marlowe's *Hero and Leander*, in contrast, was essentially a memorial, not published until five years after he was murdered. It then appeared in two versions, the first with only Marlowe's two sestiads (poetic sections: the term is derived from Sestos, where the poem takes place, on the model of *Iliad*—more properly, *Iliads*—a poem about Ilium, or Troy, composed of twenty-four books, each an Iliad), the second with an additional four sestiads by George Chapman continuing and concluding the story. In both, a section of 21 lines in the second sestiad are out of place: this work was clearly less carefully prepared for the press than Shakespeare's two narrative poems—Shakespeare himself was presumably overseeing their publication. The usual explanation for Shakespeare turning to poetry is that the theatres were closed because of plague in much of 1592–4; but this of course does not account for the character of the two poems he published, nor for the way he went about it.

For readers, Shakespeare was best known in his own time not as a playwright but as the poet of *Venus and Adonis* and *The Rape of Lucrece*; and judging from the publication history, Marlowe's *Hero and Leander* was equally widely read.[4] Let us begin as the poems begin, with their dedications. That of Marlowe's poem, addressed to Thomas Walsingham, is a publisher's dedication, not an author's. We might view this dedication as bringing two of Marlowe's worlds together: Thomas Walsingham was the cousin of Francis, the head of the Elizabethan secret service, and therefore Marlowe's spy-master. Francis died in 1590. Thomas was apparently Marlowe's patron—perhaps the undercover activities ran in the family. At the very least, Marlowe must have known Thomas through Francis. Moreover, perhaps spying and writing poetry are in this case related—we do not know that Thomas Walsingham gave Marlowe money for writing poetry; Marlowe was simply on the payroll. They were certainly close associates: Marlowe was living with Thomas Walsingham in Kent in 1593, out of London because of the plague.

The publisher Edward Blount in 1598 says he is issuing the poem as a memorial to Marlowe, but the dedication does not imply that the manuscript came to him via Thomas Walsingham; it simply says that since Marlowe had been 'accustomed... to the gentle aire of [Walsingham's] liking', Walsingham was the obvious dedicatee. Blount is not assuming he will receive anything from Walsingham except the cachet of his name. And George Chapman dedicated his continuation of Marlowe's two sestiads to Thomas Walsingham's wife, who was one of Queen Elizabeth's ladies in waiting; but Chapman's dedication says nothing about Marlowe, only that Walsingham has been Chapman's 'honoured best friend' and has shown him 'ancient kindnes', and that he therefore considers it only fit that, as the two parts of the poem are joined, the dedications should reflect the marriage; and he duly offers 'wished service'. The point of these dedications is not simply gratitude. They give the poem a sense of class, a sense that this is the world Marlowe moved in, whatever you may have heard about his shady associates and sordid death.

Now consider the Shakespeare dedications. What can we deduce about his relationship with the Earl of Southampton from that to *Venus and Adonis*? The dedication begins,

> TO THE RIGHT HONORABLE Henrie Wriothesley, Earle of Southampton, and Baron of Titchfield.
> Right Honourable,
> I know not how I shall offend in dedicating my unpolisht lines to your Lordship, nor how the worlde will censure mee for choosing so strong a proppe to support so weak a burthen, only if your Honour seeme but pleased, I account my selfe highly praised, and vowe to take advantage of all idle houres, till I have honored you with some graver labour. But if the first heire of my invention prove deformed, I shall be sorie it had so noble a god-father: and never after eare so barren a land, for feare it yeeld me still so bad a harvest, I leave it to your Honourable survey, and your Honor to your hearts content which I wish may alwaies answere your owne wish, and the worldes hopefull expectation.
>
> Your Honors in all duetie,
William Shakespeare

Shakespeare certainly is not claiming to know the Earl, let alone any intimacy with him. It is not even clear that Southampton had seen the poem before it was published—certainly there is no implication that he has given Shakespeare permission to dedicate the work to him. It sounds as if Shakespeare is doing this on spec, so to speak, with the promise that if it pays off, he will dedicate something more substantial to Southampton. This is the first printed work with Shakespeare's name attached to it. And the Earl, at the age of 19, was almost as new to this as Shakespeare was: *Venus and Adonis* was only the second poem that had been dedicated to him. The first was a Latin *Narcissus*, written by Burghley's secretary John Clapham. Southampton's father had died when his son was still a minor. Southampton became Burghley's ward, and Burghley had proposed marrying the youth to his granddaughter. Southampton refused, and paid a heavy fine for doing so. The *Narcissus* is clearly a response to that, and so may be those of Shakespeare's sonnets persuading a narcissistic youth to marry, in which case Southampton would be at least one of the young men addressed in the sonnets, though not necessarily the one Shakespeare—or rather, the speaker of the poems—falls in love with.

It has been suggested that *Venus and Adonis* is an answer to *Narcissus*, a high-minded youth giving good reasons for not falling in love with the queen of love, who is represented as the queen of whores. Colin Burrow, in his edition of the poem, argues against this, saying that the price Adonis pays, being gored by a boar and turned into a flower, is not a persuasive argument in favour of remaining a bachelor; but it *is* an argument against the queen of love, and perhaps Burrow is considering the whole question too narrowly. Can it really be the case that the poem and the dedicatee have nothing to do with each other? This is not a rhetorical question, and it makes a difference to one's reading of the poem as we consider just how embedded the work is in the realities of Shakespeare's social world.

Judging from the dedication to *The Rape of Lucrece* a year later, Shakespeare's gamble did pay off. The second dedication is significantly more enthusiastic and less cautious than the earlier one:

> The love I dedicate to your lordship is without end: wherof this Pamphlet without beginning is but a superfluous Moiety. The warrant I have of your Honourable disposition, not the worth of my untutord Lines, makes it assured of acceptance. What I have done is yours, what I have to doe is yours, being part in all I have, devoted yours. Were my worth greater, my duety would shew

greater, meane time, as it is, it is bound to your Lordship; To whom I wish long life still lengthned with all happinesse.

Your Lordships in all duety.
William Shakespeare

This poem, however, certainly seems less applicable to the young dedicatee than *Venus and Adonis* did. On the other hand, Shakespeare is not claiming that this is the 'graver labour' promised in the *Venus and Adonis* dedication. This is declared to be a fragment, a 'pamphlet without beginning', a 'superfluous moiety'—in other words, if the Earl continues being supportive, he will get . . . what? A poem on the order of *The Aeneid* or *The Faerie Queene*? In fact, there is no promise of some graver work here, just the assurance that if the patronage continues, the dedications will continue. Who gets what out of this?

Presumably the patronage in both these cases consisted in some cash payment. The poems themselves, however, imply that Shakespeare is not anticipating simply cash, but an entry into the world of aristocratic patrons and erudite readers. At least this would produce for him a less unstable audience with more clearly calculable tastes than the public theatre audience, and at best it would produce a place in some noble household, with an annuity, which was the best kind of patronal endowment. That was the kind of poet Shakespeare was trying to be: his most immediate model was a poet who has largely disappeared from literary history, Abraham Fraunce, who was attached to the Countess of Pembroke's household, and in 1592 published a long mythological poem with commentary called *The Countess of Pembroke's Yvychurch*, with a role for the Countess and its own version of the Venus and Adonis story.

But there were no more dedications to Southampton. When, at the age of 21, he came into his inheritance, it basically consisted of debts—he was, in short, not the right patron. In 1594 the theatres reopened; and Shakespeare must also have decided that this was not the kind of poet he wanted to be after all. His one other long poem, *A Lover's*

Complaint, a Spenserian elegy published with the *Sonnets* in 1609, has no dedication at all; and though for the past half century critical opinion has maintained that, despite the anomalous style, it is by Shakespeare, the most detailed computer analysis, done in 1983, is quite firm about the fact that it is not.[5] But the publisher Thomas Thorpe was equally unequivocal, heading his edition of the poem 'A Lovers complaint. *BY* WILLIAM SHAKE-SPEARE'. There is no reason to suspect any misrepresentation in this. But the manuscript of the sonnets and *A Lover's Complaint* is unlikely to have come to Thorpe from Shakespeare; and in cases where the author is not involved in a book's publication, the ascription of even a reputable publisher in the period has only limited value.

A Lover's Complaint is spoken by a forsaken woman, seduced and abandoned by an eloquent charmer—as a conclusion to the various narratives of the sonnets, it presents the betrayed poet-lover finally having turned the tables, not only on his mistress, but on all lovers. This plot begins where the sonnets end, with betrayal and frustration. As Shakespeare pursues and develops the theme in his drama, it shows the master of language and argument getting his own back, the dramatic poet avenging himself on the lyric subject. This poet says, if I can't make you love me I can make you hate me; if I can't give you life I can take it away. Dramatically, the sonnets culminate not in triumphant creativity but in relentless malice and vindictiveness—the poet of the sonnets eventuates not in Romeo or Prospero, but in Iago. The repeated lyric claim that 'my friend and I are one' achieves a dangerous dramatic reality as Iago declares to Othello that 'I am your own forever', and asserts that 'In following him I follow but myself'.

But was it Shakespeare's idea to end his sonnets in this way? To conclude a volume of sonnets with a long poem was not unusual: Spenser's *Amoretti* concludes with his own *Epithalamion*, Samuel Daniel's *Delia* with *The Complaint of Rosamond*. Thorpe may simply have felt the collection lacked a suitable ending. As for the question of authorship, critics became dubious about the matter early in the twentieth century, and remained so until the 1960s. The poem is in the same stanza form as *The Rape of Lucrece*, but includes a number of archaisms uncharacteristic of Shakespeare, and forty-nine words or forms found nowhere else in his works. This vocabulary evidence against Shakespeare's authorship has been countered by the argument that plays that are unquestionably by Shakespeare often employ new vocabulary, and include new verbs made from nouns and newly invented compound adjectives, and that therefore the unusual and unique usages may just as well indicate, on the contrary, that the poem is in fact Shakespeare's. This argument may, of course, primarily constitute evidence of how manipulable stylometric analysis can be.

Several impressive critical readings of the poem have insisted that it is both authentically Shakespearean and has an integral place among the sonnets.[6] Colin Burrow, in the most authoritative essay on Shakespeare's poems, declares discussion about the poem's attribution 'definitively ended'.[7] But consensus remains elusive: Brian Vickers, shortly after the declaration of the definitive end of discussion, ascribed the poem to John Davies of Hereford.[8] All one can say with absolute confidence is that to read the sonnets as the readers of Thorpe's quarto did—which is to say, as Shakespeare's contemporaries did—one must take *A Lover's Complaint* into account.

But, we may wish to say, it simply doesn't sound like Shakespeare. In fact, what sounds like Shakespeare has varied from age to age. In Shakespeare's own time, Robert Allott's *Englands Parnassus: or the choycest flowers of our moderne poets*, an anthology of modern poetic excerpts published in 1600, ascribes John of Gaunt's dying speech from *Richard II* to Michael Drayton, and several passages by William Warner to Shakespeare. Drayton and Warner do not sound to us like Shakespeare, but in 1600, at least to one editor, they did. Indeed, we can press further: *King John* and *The Merry Wives of Windsor* do not sound like each other, but both are Shakespeare. *Titus Andronicus* for a long time sounded so little like Shakespeare that many critics from the eighteenth to the mid-twentieth century worked hard to remove it from the canon. Nevertheless, it remained there, serving for one set of commentators as potent evidence that Shakespeare could write bad plays, and for another that since Shakespeare could not have written so bad a play, it could not be by Shakespeare. (Now, however, it has become a good play.) Shakespeare's final history play *Henry VIII* has for the last century been assumed to be a collaboration with John Fletcher, though there is no evidence to support this view except the fact that there are sections of it that do not sound to us like Shakespeare—or do not sound like what we want Shakespeare to sound like. Computer data does find Fletcher's hand in *Henry VIII*— or at least finds it for those who are looking for it—but the cautionary example of *The Elegy for William Petre*, declared by the computer to be by Shakespeare, duly included by Stephen Greenblatt in the Norton Shakespeare and by David Bevington in the Scott Foresman Shakespeare, and then, soon after, shown (not by a computer but by a careful reader with a good memory) to be by John Ford, should warn those of us who are not computer engineers to remain agnostic: the computer engineers had from the beginning declared that the program used to examine the *Elegy* was improperly designed.[9]

The dedication to the 1609 volume of the Sonnets has been a critical hornets' nest. It is designed to look like the inscription on a funeral monument:

TO.THE.ONLIE.BEGETTER.OF.
THESE.INSUING.SONNETS.
M^r.W. H. ALL.HAPPINESSE.
AND.THAT.ETERNITIE.
PROMISED.
BY.
OUR.EVER-LIVING.POET.
WISHETH.

THE.WELL-WISHING.
ADVENTURER.IN.
SETTING.
FORTH.

T. T.

What does 'the only begetter' mean? If it refers to the fair youth of the first 126 poems, it ignores the final series of poems to the mistress and *A Lover's Complaint*. Southampton's initials were H. W., and the Earl of Pembroke—one of the patrons of Shakespeare the dramatist, and a dedicatee of the first folio—was William Herbert; both of these have been proposed as Mr W.H. (Southampton with his initials erroneously reversed), but both are quite impossible: to refer to an earl as 'Mr.' was so insulting as to be legally actionable. Oscar Wilde, in his story 'The Portrait of Mr. W. H.' proposed a boy actor named Willie Hughes (his existence had earlier been suggested by the eighteenth-century classical scholar Thomas Tyrwhitt), but there is no record of any such person in Shakespeare's company or elsewhere, and even within Wilde's story the boy is deemed a fantasy. It is not even clear that 'the only begetter' means the subject of the poems: the dedication is provided by the publisher, not the poet, and it may refer simply to whoever supplied him with the manuscript. Colin Burrow, in his Oxford edition of the Complete Poems, briskly and amusingly disposes of Mr. W. H., observing that all the proposed candidates are impossible, and jocularly offers instead 'Who He?'[10] This, in fact, seems to me probably correct: the great bibliologist Arthur Freeman has suggested to me that the initials stand for 'Whoever He (may be)', and has found a parallel in a contemporary pamphlet. The dedication thus acknowledges that the publisher does not know the identity of the poems' 'only begetter'.

The original volumes of *Venus and Adonis* and *The Rape of Lucrece* have the look of books whose publication has been carefully overseen by someone thoroughly familiar with the texts—if not the author, at least a very knowledgeable surrogate. Shakespeare's sonnets are, editorially and bibliographically, another matter entirely. They were, to begin with, not a book. At least some of them circulated initially in manuscript, and the fact that these poems were first conceived as coterie literature is essential to our understanding of the nature of the book that finally materialized as *Shake-speares Sonnets*. Our evidence for their circulation in manuscript—it should be emphasized that it is our only evidence—comes from the miscellaneous writer Francis Meres, who in 1598, in *Palladis Tamia* ('Athena's Treasury', perhaps with a pun on Thames), a volume comparing London's literary scene with that of ancient Athens, praises Shakespeare's 'sugred sonnets among his private friends';[11] and while it is difficult to imagine 'sugared' applying to poems like 'They that have power to hurt and will do none' (94) or 'Th'expense of spirit in a waste of shame' (129), the adjective certainly describes many of the sonnets written to the beloved young man.

There was nothing secretive about this mode of publication; manuscript circulation was a normal mode of transmission for much lyric poetry in the period. The poet was writing for an audience he knew. The Shakespeare of the sugared sonnets is very much the Shakespeare of the social and cultural world implied by the dedications to *Venus and Adonis* and *Lucrece*; but, as Meres's reference to an audience of 'private friends' suggests, precisely because the sonnets circulated only in manuscript, their poet is far more deeply embedded in that world than Shakespeare the narrative poet is. The subtext of *Venus and Adonis* and *Lucrece* may be the search for a noble patron; but the sonnets imply a literary circle of taste and wit in which Shakespeare moves with ease. Patronage is still an issue in these poems, with the poet promising immortality to the aristocratic youth, and another poet competing for his attention; but the patronage relationship is no longer simply a matter of dedications: it is now the subject of the poems, and is intense, intimate, and even at times explicitly erotic. That sense of intimacy was shared, too, by the 'private friends'; and the social world in which the sonnets circulated was correspondingly complex and sophisticated.

It is disappointing, therefore, that none of the sugared sonnets have been found in commonplace books of the 1590s. A small number of the sonnets do appear in manuscript compilations, but all date from after the publication of Thorpe's 1609 quarto. Manuscript circulation typically involved a reciprocity between author and recipient, in the sense that the reception of manuscript poems was not passive. The gift of a poem really was a gift, its text often specifically reworked to appeal to a particular recipient; and the recipient treated it as a valued possession, copying it out—or more often having it copied by a secretary—into personal collections of favourite poems, bits of wisdom, and selections from his or her reading. Often the transcribed versions of the poems would include the recipient's own revisions, so that the poem became even more definitively the owner's, not the author's; and often as not the author's name would be indicated only by initials, or not at all. Such compilations give us a striking sense of how ambiguous the notion of literary property was in the period (whose poems are these, the author's or the recipient's?), and—especially important to emphasize—how little the circulation of literature, as opposed to its preservation, depended on the printing press.

What does it mean, then, that Shakespeare's 'private friends' survive only in Meres's report? Probably very little—certainly not that Meres was misinformed, or that none of them thought Shakespeare's poetic gifts worth preserving. The survival rate of private papers from the age is low, and Meres's claim is not in doubt. The fact that some of the poems were in fact in circulation is demonstrable from the appearance of two of the sonnets, in versions different from those of Thorpe's 1609 quarto, in a miscellaneous collection of twenty poems called *The Passionate Pilgrim* published by William Jaggard (who was to be the printer of the first folio) in 1599. The whole volume is ascribed to Shakespeare on its title page,[12] though only five of the poems included, the two sonnets and three more excerpted from *Love's Labour's Lost*, are by Shakespeare—the play had been published in 1598 with Shakespeare's name on the title page. Four other sonnets, on the subject of Venus and Adonis but obviously not by Shakespeare, nevertheless enabled Jaggard to trade on the poet's name by evoking what was at the time, and until well into the next century, his best known poem. Shakespeare clearly had nothing to do with the book's publication, though there is no reason to consider it piratical: Jaggard was publishing a manuscript that he had acquired or assembled perfectly legally, though the ascription of the whole volume to Shakespeare is clearly a misrepresentation.

The two independent sonnets, versions of Thorpe's 138 and 144, have generally been treated as earlier states of the texts, and have therefore been used as evidence—once again, the only evidence we have—of Shakespeare the lyric poet in the process of revision. This is not an inevitable assumption: Thorpe's copies certainly did not come from Shakespeare, any more than Jaggard's did, and there is no way of knowing how many intermediate versions lay between the originals and the printer's copy. Some of the differences between Jaggard's and Thorpe's versions may instead reveal the tastes of one or two of the 'private friends', revising to suit their own sense of prosody and poetic language, or even to simplify poems they found too complex. Colin Burrow's commentary is especially good on the implications of the sonnets' original mode of circulation in manuscript, where both the mystification and the playfulness that have so frustrated later readers were entirely appropriate.

How Thorpe's edition of the sonnets got into print is unclear, but there is no reason to believe that the 1609 quarto was surreptitious. Thorpe had published play quartos, including Ben Jonson's *Volpone* and *Sejanus*, and must have been known to the playwright. The text of the 1609 sonnets is on the whole an unproblematic one—these are difficult poems, but their difficulty was not introduced by the printer.

They exhibit none of the confusions of the *King Lear* quarto, which apparently derived from problems both with Shakespeare's eccentric spelling and with deciphering Shakespeare's handwriting. Thorpe's manuscript of the Sonnets was therefore presumably a fair copy, not in Shakespeare's hand.

There is only one major muddle: the opening of sonnet 146 reads

> Poore soule, the center of my sinfull earth,
> My sinfull earth these rebbell powres that thee array,

which cannot reflect difficult handwriting. Perhaps the last three words of the first line were an emendation in the margin, which carelessly became the beginning of the next line as well, thereby destroying the pentameter. There is, of course, no evidence on which to base a revision, but the history of revisions of the second line (proposals for the first foot include 'Feeding', 'Rebuke', 'Thrall to', 'Flatt'ring', 'Spoiled by', 'Lord of', and 'Pressed by') is a miniature history of changing poetic taste.

Thorpe's volume did not sell well enough to warrant a second edition. Why, given the continuing success of *Venus and Adonis* and *The Rape of Lucrece*, the sonnets were not popular in 1609 is difficult to say, but it should make us take with a grain of salt the claim that Shakespeare's name on a title page was enough to guarantee a healthy market for the book. The tantalizing evidence of emotional turmoil and illicit sex that makes them irresistible to us apparently was not a big selling point for Shakespeare's contemporaries: it was in Sidney's sonnets (which strike us as relentlessly literary) that early readers found the satisfactions of autobiography and erotic revelation. The usual explanation for the Shakespeare sonnets' neglect is that the vogue for sonnets was past; but in 1609 the vogue for Shakespeare certainly was very much alive. The sonnets in print remained what they had originally been: coterie literature, experimental, difficult and daring both linguistically and erotically, and seriously playful. The fact that their attractiveness to that coterie audience did continue is clear from the number of these sonnets that reappear in commonplace books of the period after publication: people continued to copy the ones they liked, circulate them, make them their own. The fact that the number is very small—there are twenty-five manuscript versions of only twelve sonnets out of the hundred and fifty-four—may suggest that the coterie had diminished significantly as well.[13]

There was no second edition of the Sonnets until 1640, twenty-four years after Shakespeare's death. That edition, however, involved wholesale revision. The publisher John Benson, capitalizing on the undiminished sales of *Venus and Adonis*, produced a volume of what looked to be not old-fashioned sonnets but new Shakespeare love poems. The transformation involved both format and erotics: eight are omitted entirely; many of the remaining sonnets are run together, making them 28-line poems, and all are given titles, such as 'True Admiration', 'Self-Flattery of her Beauty', 'An Entreaty for Her Acceptance'—as the latter two indicate, most of the love poems addressed to the young man are now addressed to a woman. To effect this, it was necessary only to change three masculine pronouns within the poems to feminine ones and supply a few gendered titles, but since the sonnets to the young man form a fairly consistent narrative, that was sufficient to change the story. The motive for this was probably not any nervousness about Shakespeare's sexuality; Benson simply wanted to bring the poems up to date, and thereby transformed the poems from an Elizabethan sonnet sequence to a collection of Cavalier love lyrics. The volume was properly a miscellany, including *The Phoenix and the Turtle*, poems from *The Passionate Pilgrim*, Milton's poem in praise of Shakespeare from the second folio, and pieces by Jonson, Herrick, Francis Beaumont and others.

Even this was not a great success, and there was no subsequent edition until the eighteenth century. In 1710, a supplementary volume to Nicholas Rowe's six-volume Shakespeare reprinted Benson's text, making it the first Shakespeare that could be called complete. In a competing volume issued the previous year, Bernard Lintot published the poems using the 1609 text of the sonnets; but sales of this were too small to warrant a further edition. Benson's revision remained the Shakespeare sonnets until late in the century; and indeed, these versions of the poems were still being reprinted in the nineteenth century. The definitive scholarly return to the 1609 quarto was the work of Edmond Malone, who in 1790 produced an edition that finally brought the editing of the poems in line with the editing of the plays by taking the original texts into account. It rationalized Thorpe's text, certainly, but its clarifications have on the whole stood the test of time.

In a few critical instances, however, Malone undertook wholesale rewriting to produce the kind of sense the eighteenth-century Shakespeare seemed to demand. The most significant of these involves a crux in sonnet 129, 'Th'expense of spirit in a waste of shame'. Here 'lust in action' is described, in the 1609 quarto, as 'A blisse in proofe and proud and very wo'. The line continued to read this way, with minor adjustments to modernize spelling and punctuation, throughout the next century—through John Benson's 1640 edition, Bernard Lintot's in 1709, Nicholas Rowe's in 1710, and the numerous popular editions throughout the eighteenth century, until Malone's, in which the line became 'A bliss in proof, and prov'd, a very woe'. Thereafter, with very few demurrals, this became the line: Malone was claimed to have restored Shakespeare's original.

But the emendation is almost certainly incorrect. Orthographically, the quarto's 'proud' could in 1609 be read as either 'proud' or 'provd'— though for the latter, considering the compositor's practice in the rest of the volume, 'prou'd' would have been the expected form—but, as with 'travaill' meaning both travail and travel in Shakespeare's English, the reader of 1609 who saw 'proved' in the word would not have seen only that, and would have read it as both: *provd* retained the sense of *proud*. It is a sense, in fact, that we should certainly not edit out of the poem: 'pride', says the Bible, is what 'goeth before destruction, and a haughty spirit before a fall' (Proverbs 16:18)—before the sonnet's 'very woe', before 'this hell' in which the poem ends. *Proud* also means erect, or tumescent, as in sonnet 151:

> My soul doth tell my body that he may
> Triumph in love; flesh stays no farther reason;
> But, rising at thy name, doth point out thee
> As his triumphant prize. Proud of this pride,
> He is contented thy poor drudge to be,
> To stand in thy affairs, fall by thy side.
>
> (7–12)

This is a usage still current today in the medical term 'proud flesh'. Therefore, whatever Shakespeare intended, the most we may reasonably argue is that both readings are possible; or to put it more strongly, that the two readings are not separable. It should be emphasized, however, that there is no evidence that readers before 1790 ever read the word as anything but 'proud'. Simply to eliminate one of the word's senses, as Malone's emendation does, is both to falsify the text and abolish its history.

But the transformation of 'proud' to 'proved' required Malone to make another revision in the line, less noticeable, though arguably even more radical: the change of the second 'and' to 'a', so that the clause reads not 'and proud and very wo' but 'and prov'd, a very woe'. This emendation transforms the view of sex from a tripartite act—a bliss both during action and when completed, and also true woe—to a simple before and after contrast, bliss in action, woe afterwards. There is no room for 'proud' in this neatly balanced pair. If the 1609 quarto (or Benson's 1640 volume) was the form in which Donne, Jonson, Herbert, Milton, Marvell, Dryden read Shakespeare's sonnets, Malone's poem is not the poem they read. Our Shakespeare is not Shakespeare's Shakespeare. But Malone's poem has its history too. It is now not only our poem, but the poem of Keats, Wordsworth, Browning, Yeats, Eliot, Auden. Robert Graves and Randall McLeod saw through it; but to return with them to the Shakespeare of Donne and Marvell is to abolish the Shakespeare of Keats and Yeats.[14]

Malone's Sonnets, of course, had a more problematic consequence for Shakespeare: it had the poet pining once more, in the first 126 of the poems, not for a woman but for a man; and when in 1793 the editor George Steevens explained his refusal to include the poems in his Shakespeare edition by asserting that 'the strongest act of Parliament that could be framed, would fail to compel readers into their service', it is unlikely that metaphoric complexity was what bothered him. Everyone remembers that Wordsworth said of the Sonnets that 'with this key/ Shakespeare unlocked his heart', but he also declared them 'abominably harsh, obscure, and worthless'.[15] For the nineteenth and a good part of the twentieth centuries it was customary to deal with what looks, from the perspective of the past forty years, like an overtly homoerotic sequence by arguing, when it was acknowledged at all, that the homoeroticism was purely conventional, or that the sonnets were not autobiographical—the lovestruck poet was a persona, and the sonnets to the young man no more implied that Shakespeare was gay than *Macbeth* implies that he was a murderer. Of course, claiming that Shakespeare was only a gay paedophile in his imagination probably doesn't do much to preserve his image. But in fact, recent editors have accepted the sonnets' homosexuality without worrying much about Shakespeare's, and contemporary commentary on these poems is sexually much more open than it is in similar editions of the plays.

3

Romeo and Juliet

The several iterations of *Romeo and Juliet* are especially enlightening in a study of Shakespeare's texts because they preserve the sense of the play as a process. The play was written early in Shakespeare's career, and clearly underwent considerable revision in the course of composition. Performed around 1596, it was first published in a quarto in 1597, and then in a fuller text in 1599—only the latter bears Shakespeare's name on the title page. This chapter focuses initially on a small number of moments in Q1 that make a different kind of dramatic sense from the same moments in Q2, and that seem to me thereby to give us a rather different play as a whole; and then turn to what happens when we take those alternative dramas into account in thinking about the play and undertake to produce out of them a coherent *Romeo and Juliet*. Throughout, I am concerned with the larger question of what the relation is between the texts that have been enshrined in the quartos and the folio and the play on Shakespeare's stage; and ultimately with the translation of those printed texts back into theatrical performances.[1]

For a long time the differences between Q1 and Q2, and the presumed defectiveness of Q1, were explained by invoking the concept of memorial reconstruction: Q1 was claimed to be a text put together by actors with deficient memories. But over the years the arguments postulating memorial reconstruction in Q1 looked increasingly tenuous; and they have now been effectively demolished by Paul Werstine and Lukas Erne, though both retain them to account for small individual moments.[2] But memorial reconstruction will not help with any of the problems I consider. Here is Erne's concluding summary of his argument about the relation of the two texts, which seems to me by far the best proposal, an elegant account of a very complex situation: 'Shakespeare's original script as reflected by Q2 seems likely to have been abridged before the play reached the stage, but this abridgment accounts only for a portion of the divergences between Q1 and Q2, the omissions, but not the textual differences. While the latter seem partly a matter of memorial agency, it seems possible that small-scale authorial revision also contributed a share towards them.'[3] I quote this first, because, as will become clear from a number of my examples, it seems to me in general right; but there are some interesting cases that it does not account for. My argument is not framed as a debate with Erne, but as an examination of some puzzles that Erne's edition has got me thinking about. Needless to say, I have concluded that the situation is even more complicated than his complicated formulation allows.

Let us start with the Prologue, famously a sonnet—but only in Q2; in Q1 it appears as two quatrains and two couplets. Q1 at this point was apparently the prior text, and the Prologue did not start out as a sonnet, but turning it into a sonnet was a bright second idea. Is there a point to its being a sonnet (or becoming one)? Sonnets do figure significantly elsewhere in the play, forming part of the action during the ball scene, where the lovers' dialogue is an extended sonnet, with an extra quatrain after the couplet—the first expression of their love is a sonnet, though the sonnet cannot quite contain what they have to say. (Bradin Cormack has ingeniously suggested that the extra quatrain is the beginning of a second sonnet, interrupted by the Nurse.[4]) That might suggest that making the Prologue a sonnet, introducing the love story with a sonnet, was an afterthought—perhaps considered ultimately a mistake, since it seems not to have remained in the text: the folio omits the Prologue entirely.

In both quartos the Prologue is printed in italics, but whereas Q2's Prologue is clearly part of the action, supplied with a speaker, a *Chorus*,

Q1's Prologue is printed to look like a prefatory poem. So, if Q1 is, as Erne puts it, as close as we can come to the play on Shakespeare's stage, the typography of Q1 at this point is treating the play as a book.

The two prologues prepare us for rather different plays. Q2 gives us the version that has become standard:

> *Two housholds both alike in dignitie,*
> *(In faire Verona where we lay our Scene)*
> *From aunciet grudge, breake to new mutinie,*
> *Where ciuill bloud makes ciuill hands vncleane:*
> *From forth the fatall loynes of these two foes,*
> *A paire of starre-crost lovers, take their life:*
> *Whose misadventur'd, piteous overthrowes,*
> *Doth with their death burie their Parents strife.*
> *The fearfull passage of their death-markt love,*
> *And the continuance of their Parents rage:*
> *Which but their childrens end nought could remove:*
> *Is now the two houres trafficque of our Stage.*
> *The which if you with patient eares attend,*
> *What heare shall misse, our toyle shall strive to mend.*[5]

To begin with, the dignity and the symmetry of the two families is stressed—they are 'both alike'—and this initially seems to be an aspect of 'fair Verona', one of the things that make the city decorous and beautiful. But then the dignity turns out to involve an ancient grudge, which eventuates in 'new mutiny'—a developing process is implied, and line 4 describes a continuing state of civil war. 'Civil', like 'dignity', has unexpected double senses: 'civil blood' could mean 'natural courtesy', an aspect of the dignity that makes the city fair; but by the end of the line we see that it means just the opposite, 'civic warfare'. In line 5, the 'loins' that give life to their children are 'fatal', both death-dealing and ominous or fated, and the lovers are 'star-crossed', doomed by the malignancy of their horoscopes. This bears on the question of where the ultimate responsibility for the tragedy lies—if the lovers are star-crossed, then the feuding families with their ancient grudge are star-crossed too: they are, we might say, genetically star-crossed. However badly the families behave in what is obviously a continuing tragedy, fate, the stars, their horoscopes are responsible. The lovers are 'misadventured, piteous', and their love in line 9 has a 'fearful passage': they have bad luck, and we are to pity and fear for them—this is an Aristotelian view of the nature of tragedy, as the Renaissance understood Aristotle: misadventure in the plot, pity and terror in the response, but no hero with a tragic flaw.

The play promised by the Prologue of Q1 is significantly different, and editors have more than once declared it nonsense:

> TWo houshold Frends alike in dignitie,
> (In faire Verona, where we lay our Scene)
> From civill broyles broke into enmitie,
> Whose civill warre makes civill hands uncleane.
> From forth the fatall loynes of these two foes,
> A paire of starre-crost Lovers tooke their life:
> Whose misadventures, piteous overthrowes,
> (Through the continuing of their Fathers strife,
> And death-markt passage of their Parents rage)
> Is now the two howres traffique of our Stage.
> The which if you with patient eares attend,
> What here we want wee'l studie to amend.

'Household friends' produce a quite different background for the play. 'Civil broils' are then not simply civic warfare but courteous disagreements that break into open hostility. This gives us a progression, and no ancient grudge—it does look as if Q2 is a revision. The ancient grudge is referred to later in both versions of the play, but in Q2's preliminary summary it dominates and determines the action. In Q1 the households are friends; they move from 'civil broils' to uncivil ones. Perhaps most significantly, it is only Q2 that anticipates the end of the civil strife through the lovers' death, promising an ethically satisfying conclusion. Was that really cut from Q1, not added to Q2?

What are we to make of the sudden move into the theatrical present in both texts, the reference to the two-hours' traffic of our stage? This is the only Shakespeare play that calls attention to the length of time its action is to occupy in the theatre (*The Tempest* does note that its action is taking place in real time, though the amount of real time is unclear). But Q1 can be performed in two hours, whereas Q2 would take more like three. Does Q2 begin by artificially speeding up its action by making us expect a shorter play; or is Q2 a draft that expects to be cut by an hour in the process of being prepared for the stage? Is two hours even intended as a real estimate of the play's timing, or is it simply a way of saying how the time will seem to fly?[6]

There is a second chorus-sonnet in Q2, and it constitutes one of the most baffling elements of the text, apparently a remnant of an earlier conception of the play. In Q2, the Chorus looks like part of an uninterrupted action. It comes at the beginning of what is in modern editions Act 2 (neither the quarto nor folio texts have act and scene divisions), and implies a passage of time and a series of secret meetings and stolen kisses between the first two acts—between, that is, the ball scene and the balcony scene. In the texts as we have them, however, these two scenes proceed without pause: Romeo leaves the ball, eludes his companions, and climbs into Juliet's garden, where she is, on her balcony, for the first time, sighing her heart out for him. Nor can the Chorus be projecting future action; Act 2 is also continuous—the whole point is how fast it all goes, 'too rash, too unadvised, too sudden', no time for secret meetings now or later. This Chorus is impossible in the play as we have it. It suggests an earlier version of the play more directly based on its source in Arthur Brooke's *Romeus and Juliet*, in which the wooing does cover several months—it may be relevant that the Prologue to Brooke's long poem is a sonnet. The second Chorus is almost invariably omitted in performance, since it contradicts the action (though it was included in the 1954 Renato Castellani film, with John Gielgud made up as Shakespeare reading it from the first folio, a book that appeared seven years after his death). It has no parallel in Q1, though it is, oddly, retained in the folio text. Does its presence in Q2 and F merely indicate the desire for another sonnet? It does remind us, in any case, that the texts of plays are not the plays, and that reading a book is different from going to theatre.

Even at this preliminary point, the problems with Erne's summary are evident: establishing priority between Q1 and Q2 is not a straightforward matter. Q2 retains bits of what must be a plan for the play that was subsequently abandoned, but also includes bits that look like sophistications and fine-tunings of Q1—there will be several more as I proceed. Q1 in turn in many places is clearly an edited or cut version of the text in Q2. Each of the texts is in some respects prior to the other. Complicating the situation is the fact that the manuscript behind Q2 was apparently defective in scenes 2 and 3, for which Q1 was used as the copy text. We do not at all know, however, that the problems with the manuscript were limited to this section, and additions, adjustments or revisions may have been required (or simply felt to be desirable) elsewhere as well. This script is being turned into a book; there is no reason, moreover, to assume that the reviser was Shakespeare.

Now consider the opening action. The play which has begun with a measured formal prologue at once becomes an exchange of insults between household servants, and then a brawl. Benvolio, a Montague, enters and undertakes to keep the peace, followed immediately by Tybalt, a Capulet, who starts fighting. In Q2 Benvolio's behaviour is in character with his name, 'good will'. In Q1, however, he *does not* try to keep the peace; he simply starts fighting with Tybalt. This seems more likely to imply a cut than to mean that Shakespeare subsequently, belatedly decided to make capital out of his name. Officers and citizens enter, then Old Capulet and Old Montague, with their young wives trying vainly to restrain them. And finally the prince, Escalus, 'balance', as in the scales of justice; but also the scale recalls the symmetrical households, 'both alike in dignity' and in enmity: equivalence can imply both tension and rest. The prince aborts the fight and carries off old Capulet. Old Montague asks what happened, and Benvolio's account of the quarrel is much more forthcoming in Q2 than in Q1, where he scarcely makes a gesture toward answering Montague's question—this again seems likely to indicate a cut to speed up the action, but like the cut in Benvolio's role at the beginning of the scene, it results in a significant change in his character.

Romeo is discussed before he appears. There are no cuts in Q1's version of Benvolio's speech here. Romeo enters, characterized through a dialogue that dramatizes the standard conventions of the sonnet—Romeo is established immediately as a passionate but thoroughly conventional lover. There are, however, some curious things—curious because if Q1 *is* a cut text, it is also a revised one, and things one would expect to be revised are left alone. For example, Benvolio has claimed, both to Romeo's father and again here, that he does not know what is ailing Romeo, and he now extracts the information that Romeo is in love. Benvolio asks with whom, and Romeo goes through an extended paean to his beloved's chaste unobtainability, but pointedly refuses to name her. Nevertheless when in the next scene the list of invitees to the Capulet party is produced, Benvolio seeing Rosaline's name on the list knows at once that she is the woman in question. To make sense of this, you have to invent a continuation of their conversation while they are offstage at the beginning of scene 2, during which Benvolio extracts Rosaline's name. This quite changes the dynamic between Benvolio and Romeo; it also gives us a sense that there is a lot going on in the play that we are not being told. Is that deliberate? Or shall we simply say that this all goes by so quickly in the theatre that we don't notice it—that the book is not the play? (Of course, most of what editors trouble themselves about is unnoticeable in the theatre.)

Let us pause over the list of guests invited to the ball.

> Signor Martino and his wife and daughters;
> County Anselme and his beauteous sisters;
> The lady widow of Vitruvio;
> Signor Placentio and his lovely nieces;
> Mercutio and his brother Valentine;
> Mine uncle Capulet, his wife and daughters;
> My fair niece Rosaline and Livia;
> Signor Valentio and his cousin Tybalt;
> Lucio and the lively Helena.
>
> (1.2.64–72)

This is prose in both quartos and the folio, though it is quite regular pentameter, and is now invariably printed, as I have done, as verse. Rosaline's name comes late, in the next to last line. Presumably Shakespeare included her because that is the only way to get Romeo to agree to go to the party, but the list also reveals something about her that we have not been told: she is Capulet's niece—this is in both quartos (at this point Q2 was being set from Q1, so if there was a second thought we wouldn't know it—the folio text, however, is identical). Why suddenly make Rosaline Capulet's niece? If wooing a Capulet is such a problem in the case of Juliet, why is it not an issue with Rosaline? But perhaps it is; perhaps this casts some light on Rosaline's refusal to be wooed—Romeo calls her imperviousness to him a devotion to chastity, 'She won't be hit by Cupid's arrow', making her a conventional sonnet heroine; but is it perhaps instead a quite sensible recognition that romance with the enemy family is a bad idea?

This might open up a whole back-story, in which Romeo is compulsively drawn to the enemy, a romantically suicidal streak: he is doomed not by the stars but by his perverse romantic tastes—he says it himself, viewing the aftermath of the fight at the opening, 'Here's much to do with hate, but more with love'. The two have everything to do with each other, are aspects of each other. The Italian source for the play, one of Matteo Bandello's *Novelle* (1554), includes an overt version of this hypothetical back-story: in Bandello, Romeo proposes marriage to Giulietta precisely as a way of ending the feud between the two families. The romance is public, and political, and it is defeated by the older generation's refusal to go along with this resolution of the conflict, the continuing wish for reciprocal revenge. This was the basis for Bellini's brilliant opera *I Capuleti ed i Montecchi*, which has nothing to do with Shakespeare, but as a way of viewing the plot serves as a powerful commentary on the play, opening up its very private world to its very public implications.

Returning to the list of invitees to the ball, we notice, right in the middle of line 3, that Mercutio is also on it. Capulet has said this is a list of people he loves. Mercutio is Romeo's best friend. What is Mercutio doing there? Editors make nothing of this, but surely it ought to pull us up short, just as short as learning that Rosaline is Capulet's niece. At the very least, it indicates that the two sides in the quarrel certainly are not clearly defined. It starts to look as if Q1's 'Two household friends' might not be wrong. 'From civil broils broke into enmity'—civil in the context of 'friends' needs much less explanation than it does in the context of ancient grudges. If we consider the guest list, the play is not about inveterate enmity but about friends becoming enemies and enemies becoming lovers. Here's much to do with hate, but more with love.

It hardly needs to be added that one becomes aware of all this only as one reads the play. Performances allow no time for such questions; plays are not books. But this play has become a book (or really, three books, followed by a proliferating series of derivations). Nevertheless, the printed texts are, after all, versions of the original scripts. The questions I am posing bear not on the effect of the play in performance, and on how audiences would have reacted, but on what the actors had to work with: on the nature of those scripts, and therefore ultimately on Shakespeare's imagination. It is worth adding that one characteristic of Shakespeare's imagination, in play after play, was a love of red herrings.

The play is built around set-pieces: Romeo's opening account of his hopeless love; the Nurse's reminiscence of the earthquake; the Queen Mab speech and Mercutio's obscene conjuration of Romeo; the expanded sonnet in the ballroom scene; the balcony scene; Friar Laurence's Act 2 soliloquy and meeting with Romeo; Juliet's 'gallop apace' speech; Juliet's potion speech; Romeo's speech in the tomb; Friar Laurence's interminable concluding summation; and of course the opening Chorus and Q2's inaccurate and superfluous introductory sonnet to Act 2.

The Queen Mab speech (1.4.53–95) is one of the play's great moments, though a curious point about it is how detachable this great moment is: it is nothing but a performance. It does not advance the plot, and even Romeo objects to its inclusion in the scene—'Peace, peace, thou talk'st of nothing'. It is eminently excerptible, though marginally less so in Q2 than in Q1, since Q2's version is interrupted by Romeo in the middle of a sentence.

I want to focus on some tiny moments in the speech. Here is the opening in the two quarto texts.

> *Ben:* Queene Mab whats she?
> She is the Fairies Midwife and doth come
> In shape no bigger than an Aggat stone
> On the forefinger of a Burgomaster,
> Drawne with a teeme of little Atomi,
> A thwart mens noses when they lie a sleepe.
>
> (Q1)

> *Mer.* O then I see Queene Mab hath bin with you:
> She is the Fairies midwife, and she comes in shape no bigger thē
> an Agot stone, on the forefinger of an Alderman, drawne with
> a teeme of little ottamie, ouer mens noses as they lie asleep:
>
> (Q2)

Two things are immediately noticeable: in Q1, the speech is spoken by Benvolio. The subsequent dialogue makes it clear that this is incorrect, that what has happened is that Mercutio's speech prefix has been omitted; but the usual explanation, that the compositor was pressed for space, clearly is also wrong: the first line of the speech with a speech prefix would produce a perfectly manageable line, not even as long as Mercutio's line above it. It does look as if the compositor thought the speaker was Benvolio, which is not unreasonable, since in Q1 Benvolio is present throughout the dialogue.

But now consider Q2. Benvolio's question has disappeared, and the conversation is now entirely between Mercutio and Romeo—Benvolio is present in the scene, but he has been eliminated from this part of the dialogue. More strikingly, the speech is set as prose—this is obviously wrong; the speech is quite regular blank verse; and the final three lines, which begin the next page, are set as verse. The prose here may indicate no more than that Q2's compositor needed to save space on this page; however, it often is unclear in manuscripts whether a passage is verse or prose—the telltale upper case letter to begin each verse line was on the whole not a manuscript convention, nor was the right-hand margin of prose always justified. But elsewhere in the play Mercutio does for the most part speak prose; to that extent, this is an uncharacteristic set-piece for him, and Q2's typography is in character.

The Nurse's speeches offer an interesting if confusing parallel. Both quartos set her reminiscences, which constitute her big set-pieces, in prose, though they are, like the Queen Mab speech, clearly blank verse. But the Nurse's speeches in her early scenes are also, in both quartos, set in italics, as if to indicate that what she speaks is not merely dialogue, but a different order of discourse. A servant's speech at the end of scene 3 is also set in italics. Normally it is things outside the dialogue, such as stage directions or speech headings, that are set in italics. So are foreign languages, and written communications within the dialogue, such as letters, or Capulet's party guest list (which is referred to as a letter). The Nurse's later speeches are set in roman (and the folio sets all her speeches in roman), so whatever the italics imply, they do not distinguish her as a special kind of character—speaking with an accent, for example. But they do contribute to a continuous sense of indecisiveness or arbitrariness in the process of rendering performance as text, transforming the stage's dialogue into a book, as if the play is constantly eluding or confusing the typographer, who sets passages of verse as prose, passages of roman as italic, and gives a major set-piece to the wrong character.

We return now to several tiny puzzles in Mercutio's performance, which are interesting because they are so curiously resistant to analysis. In Q1, Queen Mab is the size of an agate in a ring worn by a burgomaster—this is a measure of the fairy's smallness, but it also indicates a large agate, large enough to serve as an adornment to high civic office; a showy agate then. In Q2 the burgomaster is an alderman. A burgomaster is a civic official in a Flemish or Dutch town; alderman is the English equivalent. Neither, of course, has anything to do with Verona, but the domestication of the fantasy in Q2 seems worth noting—very literally domesticated in this case: Shakespeare's father was for a time the Stratford alderman, and subsequently the High Bailiff, the equivalent of mayor. Aldermen, then, are familiar figures, our fathers, our neighbours; whereas burgomasters are foreign, and to that extent exotic; and the Flemish and Dutch live well and like to show off. Does that part of it translate into aldermen—were aldermen notoriously showy? Was Shakespeare's father? Did he sport an agate ring? Does this tiny change, if it was Shakespeare who made it, say anything about his attitude toward his father's eminence? Was he proud of it, or perhaps a little embarrassed by his father's performance in the role? By 1596, the date of the play, his father was bankrupt, accused of usurious and fraudulent dealings; he had resigned or been removed from all his public offices, and had stopped going to church to avoid being arrested for debt. Furthermore, 1596 is also the year Shakespeare revived his father's petition for a coat of arms, a declaration that, despite his reverses, he was nevertheless a gentleman. Is there any nostalgia in the passage? Which way did the revision go? Alderman is universally adopted now, and the change may be explicable simply as an editorial clarification. But perhaps the revision went the other way: did Shakespeare perhaps have second thoughts; did alderman involve a painful nostalgia or a deep family embarrassment, safely distanced by a change to burgomaster?

There is another strange small dissonance a little further on: in Q1, Queen Mab's wagoner is 'Not half so big as is a little worm/ Picked from the lazy finger of a maid'. In Q2 the worm is 'pricked from the lazy finger of a man'. The change from picked to pricked is a change from bland and vague to vital and specific, which suggests to me that Q2's version is a revision. The change of the gender is more puzzling. Most of the figures assaulted by Mab in the speech are male—she drives over men's noses, through lovers' brains, over courtiers' knees and lawyers' fingers; but she also meddles with ladies' lips, and presses maids when they lie on their backs, 'Making them women of good carriage'—preparing them, that is, for men. The speech is largely a masculinist fantasy; hence, perhaps, the change from 'picking' to 'pricking', and the association then of pricks with men's fingers, not women's. Elsewhere, of course, Mercutio's language is notoriously phallic: 'the bawdy hand of the dial upon the prick of noon'; the threat 'to raise a spirit in his mistress' circle/ Of some strange nature, letting it there stand/ Till she had laid it and conjured it down': and especially the joke about 'that kind of fruit/ That maids call medlars when they lie alone', a joke so dirty that Mercutio's gloss, 'O that she were an open—', where 'open' is part of a word that lexicographers now assure us should have been 'open-arse', a slang term for the medlar; the word was rendered by Q1's compositor as 'open etcetera', and by Q2's 'open, or' (so that the line reads 'O that she were an open, or thou a poprin pear').

Q1's 'open etcetera' assumes we are all in on the joke; Q2 retains the smut but makes it both vague and part of a pair of genuinely pointless alternatives: O that she were an open anything, just woman defined by her openness to penetration—and this is presented as contrafactual, O that she were; if only, *magari*. But then, the fantasy continues, alternatively, O that *you* were a phallic fruit, the poppering pear. A poppering pear is a normal-shaped pear, with its phallic implications; the medlar has a soft cavity at its centre. As a pair of alternatives, Q2 presents an image of pure frustration; without the open whatever, the phallic fruit has nothing to penetrate: the poppering pear cannot be an *alternative* to the medlar; the point is that they fit together. Editors assume a misreading of something by Q2's compositor, but it is clear that Q2's printer simply missed the point (whereas Q1's compositor knows exactly what he is doing). In any case, Q2 loses the wit. Both readings register discomfort, or even embarrassment; the page has a decorum that is not incumbent on the stage. If open-arse is what Mercutio said, the joke in the theatre was not only bawdy but sexually polymorphous, with the identification now of the mistress's 'circle' with any receptive anus.

To return to the worm that is 'pricked', rather than 'picked' from the finger, in Q2 it comes from within the digit; in Q1 it is merely picked off it—the sexual implications this time are clear enough (things *come out of* pricks), and they point to masculine sex, though in this case the sex is solitary, masturbatory; hence perhaps the additional implication that laziness, whether in men or women, breeds only worms, in the body or out of it. All this of course goes by so fast in the theatre that none of these issues arise—that is, we are being told more than we can apprehend; we miss a lot, necessarily: it is too sudden, too like the lightning. The book slows us down so we can savour the poetry; but it also makes heavy weather out of wit that on stage is mercurial (or Mercutial).

Now let us consider another set-piece, Juliet's soliloquy 'Gallop apace you fiery-footed steeds' at the beginning of 3.2. In Q2 this is a major soliloquy, 31 lines long. In Q1 it is all of 4 lines. Here are the whole speech in Q1 and the opening of the speech in Q2. Though it is natural to assume that Q1 must be a cut text to speed things up on stage, the parallel lines in Q2 look like a revision:

> Q1   Gallop apace you fierie footed steedes
> To *Phoebus* mansion, such a Waggoner
> As *Phaeton,* would quickly bring you thether,
> And send in cloudie night immediately

versus

> Q2   Gallop apace, you fierie footed steedes,
> Towards *Phoebus* lodging, such a wagoner
> As *Phaetan* would whip you to the west,
> And bring in clowdie night immediately.

'Whip you to the west' has more snap than 'quickly bring you thither', and works better with 'Towards Phoebus' lodging' than with the more specific and localized 'To Phoebus' mansion'. Q2 gives a direction and an action, Q1 a destination and a conclusion. And since 25 lines later Q2's Juliet says 'I have bought the mansion of a love/ But not possessed it', this would be a reason for Phoebus' mansion to be revised out of line 2 in a later version of the speech. But did Juliet not originally have this sensational set-piece, or was it not a part of the play on the stage? It includes many of the play's most famous bits: 'Lovers can see to do their amorous rites/ By their own beauties'; 'Come, civil night,/ Thou sober-suited matron all in black,/ And learn me how to lose a winning match'; 'Come night, come Romeo, come thou day in night'; and a seriously problematic one, 'Give me my Romeo; and when I shall die,/ Take him and cut him out in little stars,/ And he will make the face of heaven so fine,/ That all the world will be in love with night . . . .' Q4 (1622) changes 'when I shall die' to 'when he shall die', but all other early texts, including the folio, read 'when I shall die'.[7] Editors in the past regularly corrected 'I' to 'he'. Recent editors, however, including Jill Levenson in the Oxford edition, retain 'I', citing the ambiguity in 'die', the common Elizabethan term for an orgasm. Levenson does not, however, explain how to interpret the passage. Can Juliet really be imagining Romeo dead, diced and stellified, in order to celebrate her first orgasm?

As an anticipation of the wedding night this set-piece would seem to provide a critical romantic context. Juliet's character deepens and matures in it (and, if 'when I shall die' is right, reveals an interestingly kinky side). It is difficult to imagine the performers wanting to truncate it, though perhaps that is the view of a reader who has lingered over the poetry—we cannot imagine it cut simply because it is so familiar. Similarly, Juliet's big final set-piece, the potion speech, a piece of bravura melodrama, is far shorter in Q1 than in Q2, 17 lines as against 43. Here again one suspects both cutting in Q1 and revision in Q2; but if Q1 is the play on the stage, were these showpieces not precisely what audiences came to hear? Perhaps in another kind of play; but speed is of the essence in this tragedy of accidents, and lingering over poetry is a luxury best indulged by readers. The potion speech in modern productions is generally felt to be an embarrassment. In Franco Zeffirelli's famous film (1968) it was replaced by just four words not by Shakespeare, 'Love give me strength'. This was presumably all Olivia Hussey could credibly manage.

As for the larger issue of the dispensability of famous set-pieces, the earliest Shakespearean prompt-books show just this sort of excision: the marked up copies of *Macbeth* and *Measure for Measure* in the first folio now in the library of the University of Padua consistently delete long passages of poetry—all Macbeth's big soliloquies are cut, all the big poetic speeches of Angelo and Claudio; passages that, for centuries of readers, have been what is most characteristically Shakespearean in these plays. But one can almost hear the stage reviser muttering 'More action and less talk', and judging from Q1 of *Romeo and Juliet*, this is how, from the beginning, Shakespeare moved from the page to the stage. So in the 1990 film of *Hamlet*, starring Mel Gibson, Zeffirelli was being authentically Shakespearean when he cut the 'To be or not to be' soliloquy—this was a surprise, and occasioned a good deal of criticism; but the biggest surprise for me was how well it worked, tightening the play and moving Hamlet toward what is, after all, the action we have been waiting for.

In fact, if *Hamlet* had not become such a canonical text we might realize that there are serious problems with the 'To be or not to be' soliloquy. At this point in the play, surely 'to be or not to be' is *not* the question; the question is revenge, an issue that is never mentioned in the speech. The question is also the reliability of the ghost that has commanded this dilatory hero to become an avenger: Hamlet himself wonders whether it is 'a spirit of health or a goblin damned'. But the speech ends by claiming that we resist suicide out of a fear of what we can never know, 'the dread of something after death,/ The undiscovered country from whose bourn/ No traveler returns . . .'. If this speech were not so ingrained in our memories we would surely find it at the very least out of place, if not incomprehensible: Hamlet has just seen his father's ghost, who has told him what happens after death: the play opens with the traveler who has returned from the undiscovered country.[8] This speech would make sense only if Hamlet delivered it *before* he sees the ghost. In fact, a 2015 London production starring Benedict Cumberbatch did open the play with the soliloquy; but there were such howls of protest from the critics that the speech was moved back (though not to its place in the familiar printed text). Actors have always revised plays to adapt them to changing conditions and new ideas—and in this case, to a really careful reading of the play— but here the text had become sacrosanct.

Let us turn now to the ending of *Romeo and Juliet*, which the stage tradition has often found deeply unsatisfactory. In both the quarto and folio texts Romeo arrives at the tomb too soon, finds Juliet apparently dead, drinks poison and dies. Forty lines later Juliet awakes, sees the dead Romeo, and mortally stabs herself. Since at least the late seventeenth century the play has been revised to give the lovers a proper farewell scene. There was even claimed to have been a Restoration version in which the lovers survived—a happy ending—though this has disappeared. In Garrick's tomb scene, however, though both lovers did end up dead, they had an extended *Liebestod*. The text was taken from Thomas Otway's 1679 adaptation, *The History and Fall of Caius Marius*, which interpolated passages from *Romeo and Juliet* into a plot derived from North's Plutarch. As one reads the Otway play now, these moments seem basically parodic—Lavinia on her balcony sighs, 'Marius, Marius, wherefore art thou Marius?' But Otway was perfectly forthright about the borrowings, and Shakespeare's original had no currency whatever on the Restoration stage—Pepys went to see the only revival, in 1662, and thought it was 'the worst [play] that I ever heard in my life, and the worst acted'.[9] In fact, *Caius Marius* was powerful and popular, and replaced *Romeo and Juliet* on the stage until Theophilus Cibber revived the Shakespeare text, more or less, in 1744. Even so, Cibber retained Otway's *Liebestod*.

There is an excellent account of the history of the play in the Restoration and the eighteenth century by George Branam, which I am relying on here.[10] Garrick produced the play in 1748, with the romantic lead Spranger Barry as Romeo. His prefatory note to the published version gives a good sense of the true afterlife of what seems to us Shakespeare's most perennially successful tragic romance:

> *The Alterations in the following Play are few, except in the last act* [that is, in the tomb scene]; *the Design was to clear the Original, as much as possible, from the Jingle and Quibble which were always thought the great Objections to reviving it.*[11]

Jingle and quibble—so much for the famous poetry and wit. Tastes change, and theatre is the great barometer of taste. For the tomb scene Garrick revised not Shakespeare but Otway—a farewell for the lovers was essential, but Otway's was too extended and took too little account of the tragic irony of the situation. So Garrick's Romeo takes the poison and then sees Juliet stir. For a moment both lovers are transported with joy, and Romeo only then recollects that he is about to expire, while Juliet, not understanding what is happening, says 'there's a sovereign charm in thy embraces/ That can revive the dead'. They die on a moment of dashed hopes, a satisfactorily romantic end. This remained the play's conclusion on the stage for a century.

There is another element in Shakespeare's text that is really not recoverable on the post-Shakespearean stage, and that has to do with both cultural attitudes toward sexuality and with the conditions of Shakespeare's theatre. Shakespeare's women were boys. In Shakespeare's source, Arthur Brooke's *Tragical History of Romeus and Juliet* (1562), Juliet is 16; Shakespeare reduces her age to 13, even insists on it (the Nurse recalls the date of her birth). This may be a nice metatheatrical touch reflecting the age of the boy playing the role, but it is also culturally significant in that Juliet has only just passed the age of consent, which in Elizabethan England, and until the eighteenth century, was 12 for women, 14 for men. The age of consent is the age at which individuals can enter into a legally binding contract, in this case the contract of marriage; that is, the age at which children no longer require parental consent to marry, the age at which they may legally elope. If this seems to us unreasonably young, Paris, pressing his case as a prospective son-in-law, even claims to Juliet's father that 'Younger than she are happy mothers made' (1.2.12). It is surely not the case that there were many 12-year-old mothers in England—Paris may only be mirroring the Elizabethan envy of supposed Italian sexual precociousness—but in Shakespeare's Verona Paris cannot be far off the mark: Juliet's mother declares that she herself was 14 when Juliet was born. And Romeo is in the throes of first love, with Rosaline and then with Juliet. For Elizabethans he would have been 15, the age at which, according to Renaissance physiology, males become sexually active.

The play, then, for Shakespeare's audience, was about a 13-year-old girl eloping with a 15-year-old boy. The romance of young love included a great deal to disturb audiences of parents with marriageable children in this patriarchal society. We inevitably miss this when the roles are played by mature, sexually secure, adults—in the 1936 film, Norma Shearer's 36-year-old Juliet and Leslie Howard's 40-year-old Romeo did not seem preposterous only because the play was a classic and these were famous and glamorous stars; the play was not a play, it was a 'vehicle', and all references to Juliet's age were removed. Two centuries earlier Theophilus Cibber's Romeo had as his Juliet his own 15-year-old daughter—her age was right enough, but Romeo was literally old enough to be her father. Garrick was a mature 33 when in 1750 he reluctantly first played Romeo; his Juliet, the Irish actress George Anne Bellamy, was 23. The 1996 Baz Luhrman film with a teenage Claire Danes and Leonardo di Caprio did capture some of the youthful transgressiveness of the original; and Franco Zeffirelli's Olivia Hussey and Leonard Whiting inhabited their roles beautifully, though there were long stretches of Juliet's part that were cut, presumably because they could not be played convincingly by a modern 16-year-old—to say nothing of a modern 13-year-old. How effective the play can be when Juliet is played as (though not by) a 13-year-old is discussed in my essay 'Shakespeare all'italiana'.[12]

We all come to these plays as readers; no matter how many productions we have seen, our opinions about what is essential derive from generations, centuries, of editorial and critical history. And as the case of the Cumberbatch *Hamlet* demonstrates, so do the productions themselves. If it is true, as Lukas Erne says, that Q1 of *Romeo and Juliet* is as close as we can come to the play on Shakespeare's stage, it has to be added that 'as close as we can come' is not very close. The book is not the play; and many plays may be derived from the surviving texts of *Romeo and Juliet*, all of them different, and all of them *Romeo and Juliet*.

4

Hamlet

In 1589 Thomas Nashe, in his preface to Robert Greene's romance *Menaphon*, sneered at playwrights who 'run through every arte and thrive by none, to leave the trade of *Noverint* [scrivener],[1] whereto they were borne, and busie themselves with the indevors of Art, that could scarcelie latinize their neckeverse if they should have neede'— prisoners condemned to be hanged could save their necks by reading a Latin verse, thus showing that they were literate; but these playwrights were not even that literate in Latin. Nevertheless, Nashe continues,

> English *Seneca* read by candle light yeeldes manie good sentences, as *Bloud is a begger*, and so foorth: and if you intreate him faire in a frostie morning, he will affoord you whole *Hamlets*, I should say handfulls of tragical speaches.[2]

Uneducated playwrights find plenty of good Senecan effects in translation; and the particular example is *Hamlet*, which Nashe finds especially egregious. There was, then, a *Hamlet* being performed in 1589 that recalled Seneca—the *Hamlet* familiar to us dates from 1600 or 1601, and a version was published in 1603 (the first quarto). The old play must have been popular, since according to the theatre manager Philip Henslowe's records, it was still being performed in 1594; and the novelist Thomas Lodge, in 1596, recalls 'the ghost which cried so miserably at the Theator, like an oisterwife, Hamlet, revenge'.[3] This gives a sense of how heavy-handed the supernatural apparatus must have been in the old play (the line does not appear in the first quarto *Hamlet*).

The old *Hamlet* was credited to Thomas Kyd because Nashe says that its author was born to the trade of *noverint*, scrivener—Kyd's father was a scrivener—and later in the passage says the author is one of those who 'imitate the Kidde in *Aesop*', suggesting that he is another kid, or Kyd. A case has also been made that it is a very early version of the play by Shakespeare, surviving in some form in Q1.[4] Nashe's evidence must then be argued away, but Nashe may have been mistaken about the play's authorship. It is true that the very loose verse of Q1 *Hamlet* sounds nothing like that of early Shakespeare, which is very formal (it also does not sound like Kyd's verse); but that may only be because this is a reported text of the sort Thomas Heywood deplored, 'copied onely by the eare',[5] and that Tiffany Stern describes in 'Sermons, Plays and Note-Takers'.[6]

Nashe's principal charge, however, is of Latin illiteracy. Did Kyd—or Shakespeare—read his Seneca in translation? Many years later Ben Jonson, the most learned of English poets, would write of Shakespeare that he had 'small Latin and less Greek'—did Kyd's or Shakespeare's Latin not extend as far as the Seneca studied in school? In that case, the putative playwright's Seneca was the Seneca of Jasper Heywood and the other translators published by Thomas Newton in *Seneca His Tenne Tragedies, Translated into Englysh* in 1581.

Hamlet appears to us more ruminative than declamatory, but that is largely a consequence of our way of performing it. When Hamlet delivers his soliloquies on the modern stage he does so as if he is thinking aloud, speaking only to himself. In the beautiful 1948 film, Laurence Olivier's Hamlet remained lost in thought while he recited the soliloquies in a voice-over. But soliloquies in Shakespeare's theatre would have been delivered from the front of the stage, addressing the audience directly. The Hamlet of 1601 did not think his soliloquies, he declaimed them, justifying himself, persuading the audience of the rightness of his cause and the wickedness of his enemies. Indeed, he accuses himself of overdoing it, 'cursing like a very drab'. If we think about performing styles, the declamatory Seneca is manifest throughout Shakespeare's career, not merely in the early *Henry VI* and *Richard III*, but in the tremendous invective of *King Lear* and *Coriolanus*, the passion of *Othello*, both Prospero's rages and his philosophizing.

The first quarto of *Hamlet* is not simply a cut version of the play familiar to us. Two of the characters have different names: Polonius is Corambis, Reynaldo is Montano. It includes a whole scene that did not remain in the play, between the queen and Horatio, in which the queen asserts her innocence and resolves to become Hamlet's accomplice in the murder of Claudius—in the standard texts, we never learn whether the queen was implicated in the death of the old king; here she twice explicitly denies it. Nor do we know whether she and Claudius were committing adultery while old Hamlet was alive; but in Q1 Claudius declares himself 'adulterous' (fol. G1v).

The title page asserts that the play was performed both in London and in the two universities of Oxford and Cambridge. If we press on these claims, however, they become problematic. The Globe was not in London but across the river on the south bank, and public theatres were explicitly forbidden in London after 1594. Is the title page therefore evidence that the first quarto derives from the text of the ur-*Hamlet*, which we know was in existence in the early 1590s? But theatrical performances by professional companies were explicitly forbidden in the universities too, so the claim about Oxford and Cambridge can at most mean that the King's Men performed in the university towns. Even this is puzzling, not to say dubious, since the Oxford Town Council repeatedly went on record during this period banning public performances of plays within the city limits. Were there exceptions that are not recorded, or did the actors manage to get around the ban somehow (e.g., performing in some gentleman's house), or did they set up their stage somewhere just outside the city limits? Or is the title page's claim simply a fabrication designed to add topographical and academic prestige to a popular play?

The text of Q1 is closer to the play on the stage than that of the second quarto. When the Ghost appears in the Queen's bedchamber, the stage direction is '*Enter the ghost in his night gowne*'[7]—modern productions generally have him, preposterously, still in the armour of his first scene, quite inappropriate for indoor wear. Ophelia—in this text Ofelia—in her mad scene is '*playing on a Lute, and her haire downe singing*'.[8] The folio text, though it is probably still too long to be the performing text, also includes bits of stage business: the 'rogue and peasant slave' soliloquy includes a cry of 'O vengeance', which is not in the second quarto and, as a two-word exclamation interrupting the blank verse, looks like a climax added by the tragic actor. And at Hamlet's death in the folio, 'The rest is silence' is followed by a histrionic 'O, o, o, o'.

Hamlet opens with a ghost, but in a way it is full of ghosts. There was, to begin with, that earlier play about Hamlet, popular around 1590—possibly an earlier version of this play, and thus an earlier play of Shakespeare's than any that survives; or possibly a popular play by one of the playwrights of the 1580s from whom Shakespeare learned his craft. This was a blood-and-thunder tragedy that, judging from Thomas Lodge's quip, became a running joke about the conventions of the form. Lodge gives a sense of how heavy-handed the supernatural apparatus must have been in the old play; he also gives a sense of how difficult it was to take seriously. For Shakespeare to have used so famous and popular a play only about ten years later, or to have rewritten his first big success, argues considerable self-confidence. But Shakespeare did more than that: he took a tragedy that had become farcical and transformed it into his most philosophical drama. We have the testimony of Gabriel Harvey that 'The younger sort takes much delight in Shakespeares Venus, & Adonis: but his Lucrece, & his tragedie of Hamlet, Prince of Denmarke, have it in them to please the wiser sort'.[9] The note has been dated to 1600–1 (that is, before the play was in print in any form); the wiser sort were therefore audiences, not readers. But this presumably does not imply university productions. Theatre in the universities was maintained as an academic prerogative, part of the educational system; the actors were students and dons, the plays were classic or neo-classic texts. It is clear what kind of imprimatur is being claimed by Q1 for this play, but it is much less clear whether the imprimatur is reliable.

Shakespeare's awareness of the problems of taking the old play seriously is revealed precisely in those moments when Hamlet himself is unable to take the ghost seriously, and makes fun of the conventions of revenge plays. 'You hear this fellow in the cellarage' (the area under the stage); 'well said, old mole' (1.5.162): this is Shakespeare, or Hamlet, playing any heckling theatregoer; and it involves, dramatically, a startling breach of decorum. This is his dead father he is playing with. How do you address your dead father? How do you talk to a ghost? But even more problematic, how seriously can you take a theatrical ghost? This is a measure of the playwright's self-confidence: Shakespeare is by 1601 very successful; he had been for three or four years the most popular dramatist writing in England, and has no need to play it safe.

But Shakespeare's use of the old *Hamlet* also argues extraordinary self-consciousness, particularly about the theatre. There are many places where he clearly is playing with his audience's awareness of the old blood-and-thunder drama, breaking the stage illusion to force on the attention of the spectator the dramatic background, the theatrical medium and even its supernatural gimmickry. When Hamlet says of the ghost, 'You hear this fellow in the cellarage' he is reminding his audience of how ghosts materialize in the theatre—this Elsinore castle is a stage with a trapdoor—and more to the point, insisting that Hamlet the character is as aware of this as his audience is. Thus the ghost of the old play is laid to rest. Hamlet does the same thing with more serious effects when, a number of times during the action, he talks of himself as an actor with a role he must perform, or as a character trapped in a play.

The first quarto text includes rudimentary versions of the famous speeches. Here, for example, is the 'To be or not to be' soliloquy, which in this text comes much earlier in the play, immediately after Corambis recounts to the king Ofelia's interlude with the apparently lovesick Hamlet:

> *Ham.* To be, or not to be, I there's the point,
> To Die, to sleepe, is that all? I all:
> No, to sleepe, to dreame, I mary there it goes,
> For in that dreame of death, when wee awake,
> And borne before an euerlasting Iudge,
> From whence no passenger euer retur'nd,
> The vndiscouered country, at whose sight
> The happy smile, and the accursed damn'd.
> But for this, the ioyfull hope of this,
> Whol'd beare the scornes and flattery of the world,
> Scorned by the right rich, the rich curssed of the poore?
> The widow being oppressed, the orphan wrong'd,
> The taste of hunger, or a tirants raigne,
> And thousand more calamities besides,
> To grunt and sweate vnder this weary life,
> When that he may his full *Quietus* make,
> With a bare bodkin, who would this indure,
> But for a hope of something after death?
> Which pusles the braine, and doth confound the sence,
> Which makes vs rather beare those euilles we haue,
> Than flie to others that we know not of.
> I that, O this conscience makes cowardes of vs all,
> Lady in thy orizons, be all my sinnes remembred.
>
> (fol. D4v–E1r)

This Hamlet comes to conclusions quite opposite to those of the Hamlet of the standard text. 'The undiscovered country' produces a smile; this Hamlet has 'a hope of something after death', rather than the dread of the Hamlets of 1605 and 1623. Is this the fault of memorial reconstruction, with the actor (obviously not the actor playing Hamlet) imperfectly remembering the speech; or is this a member of the audience trying to write it all down and producing only an approximate version of the soliloquy, which, moreover, misses its point? Or is the gist of the speech correct, and did Shakespeare, over the decade, change his attitude to the afterlife? This version of the speech is more straightforward and pragmatic about what is bad about being poor than the standard version: instead of 'the proud man's contumely', 'the insolence of office', etc., we get 'Scorned by the right rich, the rich cursed of the poor'. The poetry has gone, too: no taking arms against a sea of troubles; and there are no alternatives being debated here, no wondering whether "tis nobler in the mind to suffer', etc. But the physicality remains firmly in view: 'to grunt and sweat under this weary life'.

The 'To be or not to be' soliloquy has become the most famous speech in Shakespeare, not least because it is so eminently detachable from its dramatic context. Judging from its placement in Q1, it seems to have moved around in the play—indeed, as I have indicated, it would make the best sense only if it were spoken before Hamlet sees the ghost, that traveller from the undiscovered country who tells Hamlet what the speech says we can never know, what happens after death. Was the speech even originally written for this play? How has 'To be or not to be' become the question? Surely the questions Hamlet is confronting are the validity of revenge and whether to trust the ghost, two things never touched on in the speech.

This soliloquy as it appears in Q1 is much less like intellection and much more like a direct address to the audience—'Aye, there's the point'. Also, nothing leads up to the soliloquy itself, which requires a very presentational mode of performance: a solo performer comes to the front of the stage and delivers his speech, less as part of a dramatic fiction than as a solo performance. The relation between actor and audience is essentially unmediated here. Nor are the boundaries of the scene those we are used to: Hamlet enters while the King and Queen and Corambis are still on stage—his entrance is their cue to exit, and their dialogue continues for some moments before they depart.

Some things in the first quarto are clearly versions of the play we are familiar with: the Player's Pyrrhus speech is identical to the speech in the later texts; the play within the play is in part identical to the text of the second quarto and folio, but it also includes different passages written in excellent, very formal verse, unlike most of Q1. These are not evidence of a failure of some actor's memory, or some reporter's haste. They point rather to the involvement of an editor-poet with access to at least some part of a proper text, preparing the play for publication. At the same time, there are bits that look like improvisation in a live performance. Q1's Hamlet himself quotes the punch lines of several old gags to the players:

> And then you haue some agen, that keepes one sute
> Of ieasts [jests], as a man is knowne by one sute of
> Apparell, and Gentlemen quotes his ieasts downe
> In their tables, before they come to the play, as thus:
> Cannot you stay till I eate my porrige? and, you owe me
> A quarters wages: and, my coate wants a cullison:
> And your beere is sowre

(fol. F2r–v)

This seems to be the actor clowning—just what Hamlet warns the visiting players against.

One perennial problem in the standard text of the play that is resolved in Q1—or perhaps simply eliminated from it—is the question of Hamlet's age. Throughout the early scenes he seems very young, moody and impulsive; but then in the Gravediggers' scene Yorick's skull is said to have been in the earth for twenty-three years, and Hamlet remembers being carried on his back as a child, which would make Hamlet about thirty. Why then is he still at university? Q1, however, has Yorick's skull in the earth for only twelve years, which would make Hamlet still a teenager. Is this the actors or the editor resolving a puzzle, or during the course of revision was Hamlet belatedly made older to increase his *gravitas*? But the main thing missing from Hamlet himself in Q1 is the issue of delay and procrastination, doubting the ghost. In this text, failing to kill Claudius in the chapel scene seems less like a rationalization. This Hamlet is more active, more irrational, and much younger.

However problematic the text of Q1 is, it cannot be a pirated edition, since the King's Men gave the same publisher, Nicholas Ling, the text that became Q2. If Q1 represents the old play in some form, it means that Shakespeare began his career writing big rhetorical tragedy. One central element of the *Hamlet* of 1601 that is simply not recoverable is Shakespeare's audience's awareness of the old drama. If we keep this sort of theatrical background in mind, some parts of the play come much more clearly into focus. For us inevitably Q1 is a radically inaccurate text, including only three of the four famous soliloquies, and even these are present in garbled versions. It is, like a number of plays surviving from the 1580s and 1590s, a text of the play that the author no longer controls. But it is also, therefore, a play full of ghosts, the ghosts of what we expect because of our familiarity with the standard texts. Of course, whatever version is performed for modern audiences will be informed by the ghosts of all those other versions, the ghosts of what is left out, or in the rare case of a 'complete' version, of what we expect to be left out. And this was certainly true of the play for its original audiences, who would still have remembered that other *Hamlet*, the play popular around 1590, only ten years earlier; English Seneca, in which the ghost cried like an oyster wife 'Hamlet revenge'.

The old *Hamlet* was traditionally ascribed to Thomas Kyd, largely because of the *noverint* reference, but also because of its putative similarity to the most famous of Elizabethan revenge plays, *The*

Spanish Tragedy. *The Spanish Tragedy* was a warhorse of a play, first produced in the 1580s (but presumably before 1588, since it makes no reference to the Armada), with a great deal of blood-curdling rhetoric and many murders. It was the second part of a two-part play (following *The First Part of Hieronimo or the Spanish Comedy*)—the first part dropped out of the repertory, and survives only in a partly parodic version for a children's company published in 1605, the text of which seems to be a version produced either by memorial reconstruction or by auditors transcribing what they heard. *The Spanish Tragedy*, however, was continually revived and revised. Ben Jonson in 1601 was paid to write new speeches for it, perhaps precisely to cash in on the success of Shakespeare's revised and revived revenge drama. *The Spanish Tragedy* was bombastic, but it was also very prestigious, a popular modern classic. Getting Jonson to provide new scenes for it was something like asking Francis Ford Coppola to make some new scenes for a revival of *Gone With the Wind*—not an inconceivable idea.

Here is the most famous of Hieronymo's passionate soliloquies. He has just discovered the body of his murdered son, hanged in an arbour. During the course of the speech, the identity of the murderers is revealed to him by a letter dropped before him by his son's mistress Bel-Imperia. She witnessed the murder, and was then kidnapped and imprisoned by the murderers. She wrote the letter in her own blood (a stage direction reads 'red ink'), and drops it from the gallery above the stage—a terrific bit of theatrical business:

> O eyes, no eyes, but fountains fraught with tears;
> O life, no life, but lively form of death;
> O world, no world, but mass of public wrongs,
> Confused and filled with murder and misdeeds;
> O sacred heavens! if this unhallowed deed,
> If this inhuman and barbarous attempt,
> If this incomparable murder thus

Of mine, but now no more my son,
Shall unrevealed and unrevengèd pass,
How should we term your dealings to be just,
If you unjustly deal with those that in your justice trust?
The night, sad secretary to my moans,
With direful visions wake my vexèd soul,
And with the wounds of my distressful son
Solicit me for notice of his death;
The ugly fiends do sally forth of hell,
And frame my heart with fierce inflamèd thoughts;
The cloudy day my discontents records,
Early begins to register my dreams
Eyes, life, world, heavens, hell, night and day,
See, search, show, send, some man, some mean, that may—
              A letter falleth.
What's here? A letter? Tush, it is not so!
A letter written to Hieronymo!
'For want of ink, receive this bloody writ. *<Red ink.>*
Me hath my hapless brother hid from thee.
Revenge thyself on Balthazar and him,
For these were they that murderèd thy son.
Hieronymo, revenge Horatio's death . . .'.

                                       (3.2.1–30)

This play set the style for revenge tragedy during the early years of Shakespeare's career. Hieronymo's soliloquy gives us a good sense of where Shakespeare is coming from, as well as of how different that theatrical device the soliloquy was in Shakespeare's theatre from what it is in ours. The speech is formal and balanced; it works like a logical argument, and the principles of classical rhetoric are behind it. Like the Hamlet of the 'To be or not to be' soliloquy, Hieronymo uses a debater's tactics, or a courtroom lawyer's, to persuade his audience and win his case. This is an important characteristic of Elizabethan drama: the arts of persuasion are central to the style, and being in the audience is like listening to a debate, in the sense that your judgment is involved. You are not passively watching an action, but must decide who is right and wrong, and at critical moments Elizabethan plays characteristically stop the action and undertake to persuade you of the justice of one or another of their causes. When Hamlet declares himself a rogue and peasant slave, he does so for us as if he is thinking aloud. But Hieronymo here emotes and argues, justifying the revenge that provides the drama's climax. Revenge is an essential motivation in Elizabethan tragic drama; this is an ever-present ghost. Revenge is not an acceptable motive for Christian societies: God says that retribution is his business—'Vengeance is mine, saith the Lord'. But what was forbidden in society was regularly played out on stage.

Does the unusual length of the surviving *Hamlet* imply that the old play was a ghost that proved impossible for Shakespeare to exorcise, so that he therefore could not let go of the play and consider it finished? The folio text is shorter than that of the second quarto, but by only about 75 lines (Q2 has about 150 lines missing from F, including Hamlet's final soliloquy 'How all occasions do inform against me', but F has about 75 lines missing from Q2); and the folio includes a couple of extended passages (Hamlet's early exchange with Rosencrantz and Guildenstern including the 'Denmark's a prison' sequence, and the discussion with the players about the popularity of the 'little eyases', the children's theatre companies) that look as if they must have been cut from some earlier version, and are in any case easy to dispense with. In fact, the presence of these passages in the folio text is a puzzle. They look like cuts that would have been made at the beginning of the century. Shortly after King James came to the throne in 1603 he became the acting company's patron (which therefore was no longer the Lord Chamberlain's Men but was now the King's Men). James's queen was a Danish princess, and the critique of Denmark must have seemed at the very least impolitic. As for the deletion of the exchange about the children's companies, that too was an issue early in the century and might have been cut to avoid offending the aristocratic audiences of the rival troupes. By the time the folio text was being prepared, the queen was dead, and the children's companies had long ceased to be a problem for the adult actors. Restoring these cuts is essentially preserving the play's textual history. But in other respects, the folio text looks more like an acting text than that of the second quarto does.

Though it is the most famous Shakespeare play, *Hamlet* is also the least characteristic one. It is unusually long: almost 4,000 lines, which is twice as long as *Macbeth*, and 1,000 lines longer than the average Shakespeare tragedy. Whatever the normal performing time for an Elizabethan play was—presumably anything between two and three and a half hours—to do *Hamlet* complete, with no intermission, takes about five hours. This means that the text we have of *Hamlet* would never have been performed complete in Shakespeare's theatre (modern 'complete' texts are typically amalgams of the second quarto and folio versions, and are therefore even longer). The title role, too, is by far the largest in Shakespeare, and really unsuited to a repertory company—it is one of only three Shakespearean roles that are more than 1,000 lines long, and seem to have been written for a star (the other two are Richard III, and, interestingly, Iago—Henry V almost makes it at 999 lines—but even those roles are a quarter to a half shorter than the role of Hamlet).

Modern productions generally cut the text radically, not only to shorten the performance but also to revise the hero. In the famous 1948 film, Laurence Olivier spoke only about two-thirds of Hamlet's lines. Most of the sarcastic and manic passages were jettisoned, and Hamlet became a contemplative philosopher. In Shakespeare's text he *is* a contemplative philosopher, but only intermittently, between bouts of antic disruptiveness; and the disruptive antics really are essential to the play—they are what frighten Claudius about Hamlet, not his philosophical musings. Franco Zeffirelli's 1991 film, starring the quintessential action hero Mel Gibson, with Paul Scofield as a muted and moving ghost, daringly cut the most famous speech in the play, the 'To be or not to be' soliloquy, moving Hamlet toward the revenge that we have, after all, been told is the point of the play. Kenneth Branagh's 1996 version was touted as including the full text, but in fact it included a good deal more, not only elaborate and extended special effects for the ghost and the final scene, but added pantomime scenes, for example of Hamlet and Ophelia in bed making love (but have they really been lovers, or is this only what Polonius fears?), and additional roles enacting the Player's speech in pantomime, for John Gielgud as Priam and Judi Dench as Hecuba: were they included only so that this bloated film could boast an all-star cast? Our *Hamlet* is both more and less than Shakespeare's.

5

King Lear

King Lear survives in two versions, in a 1608 quarto and the folio. The quarto has been identified as deriving from Shakespeare's holograph—that is, the play as it was delivered to the acting company, before it was prepared for performance. Its title page has first Shakespeare's name in large letters, then the title, a summary of the added subplot of Gloucester and Edgar, and then the information that the play was performed before the King during the Christmas season. The text has idiosyncratic spellings, and the handwriting was evidently difficult to read. The printers, moreover, were apparently inexperienced, and many corrections—some erroneous—were made during the course of production. According to Kenneth Muir,

> Twelve copies exist [of the 1608 quarto], but these are in ten different states because proof-reading was carried on simultaneously with the printing. Corrections were made in the formes [the typeset pages] after the printing had begun, and corrected sheets were bound up with uncorrected sheets. The total number of variants in the twelve extant copies is 167, though some of the emendations were incorrect.[1]

The folio preserves a corrected and cut version of this quarto. It deletes about 300 lines of the text, but adds about 100 lines not in the quarto. It is in every way a clearer text, but also significantly shorter. Editors tend to prefer the quarto text because it gives us more Shakespeare, but emend it according to the folio, thereby, as in the case of *Hamlet*, producing a text that is a hybrid, and thus both much longer and different from anything audiences or readers of Shakespeare's age could have experienced.

Here is an extreme example of the relation of the quarto and folio texts: a phrase that in the folio is 'a dog's obeyed in office' is rendered in the quarto 'a dog so bade in office' (1608: 4.5.153–4; 1623:4.5.156–7), revealing either Shakespeare's idiosyncratic spelling and word spacing, and the compositor's difficulty interpreting them, or perhaps an auditory error on the part of a transcriber. But correction was erratic and incomplete: both texts retain bits that look like Shakespeare changing his mind without changing the line. At the beginning of 1.5 Kent is sent with 'letters' 'to Gloucester': 'Go you before to Gloucester with these letters.' These turn out in the next clause, however, to be a single letter addressed not to Gloucester but to Regan: 'Acquaint my daughter no further with anything you know than comes from her demand out of the letter' (1608 and 1623: 1.5.1–3). Editors (myself included) are reduced to explaining that Regan's castle must therefore be in the *city* of Gloucester, which has not been mentioned before and is never mentioned again. This strikes me as a dubious explanation, despite my complicity in it—'Gloucester' in the play never means anything except the Earl of Gloucester. It seems to me much more likely that Shakespeare's first idea was to have Lear send a packet of aggrieved letters to the Earl of Gloucester including one for him to deliver to Regan, and then changed his mind without changing the line. In any case, if the topographical explanation is correct, it is a point that is impossible to convey in anything but a footnote: on stage, the reference to Gloucester will remain a puzzle.

In performance this goes by so quickly that it is probably unnoticeable, but the play has become literature, and readers pause over things they do not understand. There are deeper puzzles in the play as well: in the opening exchange between Gloucester and Kent, Lear's division of the kingdom is discussed. Gloucester says it is to be divided evenly between Lear's two sons-in-law, implying that this plan is settled and generally known. But as the scene continues, Lear proposes distributing the kingdom in thirds to his three daughters, and demands professions of love from them. This change of plan should come as a considerable surprise—at the very least, it is evidence of Lear's radical unreliability—but nobody comments on it, and it goes by in performance (and in most editions) unnoticed. But did Shakespeare simply change his mind?

And of course the biggest surprise would have been the ending. In all the sources, historical as well as literary, Lear reclaims his throne (in some versions Cordelia commits suicide, but in others, she too survives). It was Shakespeare who changed the ending, which would have surprised or even shocked those members of the original audiences who knew the history, or had read the version of the story in Geoffrey of Monmouth, Holinshed, *The Mirour for Magistrates*, *The Faerie Queene*, or had seen or read the earlier play on the subject *The True Chronicle History of King Leir*, which was Shakespeare's immediate source. (The added subplot about the Duke of Gloucester and his two sons comes from Sidney's *Arcadia*). Imagine a play about the American Civil War in which the Union is defeated, the south secedes, and slavery is not abolished—this is not true to history, but you could hardly leave it at that. It would give you quite a lot to think about. What was Shakespeare's point in so clearly violating his audience's expectations—expectations, moreover, that the play itself raises, in the sense that by the conclusion, all the villains are dead, and the Duke of Albany's forces are victorious.

Nahum Tate's Restoration version, *The History of King Lear, A Tragedy* (1681) which 'corrects' the ending, has earned contempt from critics beginning with Addison, but it is worth taking seriously because it does address real problems in the play, things the folio's revision ignores.[2] It was admired by Samuel Johnson, not only because it was true to its sources but even more because he found Shakespeare's ending too painful, which is surely to his credit as a critic. Tate revises in ways we easily understand, even if we do not like them, clarifying, supplying motivations, justifying action, generally neatening and redirecting the play, particularly through an added romantic plot: Cordelia and Edgar are lovers. In the original play, it is unclear how we are to take Cordelia's behaviour at the opening, refusing to play her father's game. Has she behaved badly? Unless her reply to the abject Lear's recognition in Act 4 that she has cause for resentment, 'No cause, no cause' (4.7.75), is taken to be routine courtesy, it is surely an acknowledgment that there is something to apologize for. After all, the issue is not only Cordelia's love for Lear, but even more Lear's love for Cordelia. She knows he loves her best; she also knows his frailty and irascibility. In Tate, Cordelia's rudeness at the opening is strategic, designed to prevent her father from marrying her off. Tate explains, "'Twas my good Fortune to light on one Expedient to rectifie what was wanting in the Regularity and Probability of the Tale, which was to run through the whole A *Love* betwixt *Edgar* and *Cordelia*, that never chang'd word with each other in the Original. This renders *Cordelia's* Indifference and her Father's Passion in the first Scene probable.' Edgar's disguise thus becomes 'a generous Design that was before a poor Shift to save his Life'.[3] In this way, motivations that are obscure in Shakespeare are supplied with a focus.

The folio text itself is a revision, but it seems not to be Tate's sort of revision. Things one would think any reviser would want to clarify or edit out go unchanged. It is useful, therefore, to start with the folio's alterations to the quarto. What, to the earliest editors, was unsatisfactory about the play, and what constituted fixing it? Obvious errors of transcription in the quarto are corrected in the folio; and modern editors, who generally prefer the quarto text, almost invariably accept the folio readings at these points. Some things in the quarto seem like false starts, afterthoughts, unreconciled changes of mind, or just plain muddles. I have already cited the contradictory proposals for the division of the kingdom, and the ephemeral 'letters to Gloucester' which turn into a letter to Regan. In 2.1, the letter has been delivered by Kent, and has prompted Regan and Cornwall to leave their castle and go to Gloucester's—we do not see the letter being delivered, but Kent has followed them, and in the next scene Regan and Cornwall recognize him as Lear's messenger. The puzzling scene with Kent berating Oswald follows, in which, when Cornwall questions the two, Kent refuses to defend himself, allows Oswald to give all the explanations, and is deliberately, pointlessly, rude to Cornwall. Left to spend the night in the stocks, Kent then produces a letter from Cordelia, 'Who hath most fortunately been informed/ Of my obscurèd course.' This is the only indication of a continuing communication between Kent and Cordelia, which is obviously quite essential to the plot.

The folio revision clarifies none of this. The only significant change to these scenes is in Gloucester's protest against putting Kent in the stocks. In the quarto, Gloucester says 'His fault is much, and the good king his master/ Will check him for't', and there follows a direct criticism of Cornwall:

> Your purposed low correction
> Is such as basest and contemned'st wretches
> For pilf'rings and most common trespasses
> Are punished with.[4]
>
> (1608: 2.2.139–42)

That is, you don't do this to a gentleman. In the folio, both the assurance of a royal punishment and the reproach are removed, and the only sanction that remains from the quarto is the danger of angering the king:

> The king his master needs must take it ill
> That he, so slightly valued in his messenger,
> Should have him thus restrained.
>
> (1623: 2.2.141–3)

The changes make Gloucester both less naïve and more cautious in his treatment of Cornwall—this seems, like many of the folio's revisions, designed to effect a minor adjustment in character.[5] Why were the plot muddles left alone? A nicely postmodern line might be that they were considered desirable, even essential, so that the play resisted elucidation, a 'dark conceit', as Spenser says *The Faerie Queene* is. I like the muddles, and the sense they give that more is going on in the action than the play reveals; but as an explanation, this again strikes me as unlikely: when Shakespeare wants to be obscure he is quite straightforward about it, as in *The Phoenix and the Turtle*, and many passages in *Macbeth*, *Cymbeline*, *The Winter's Tale*. It seems to me more likely that the process of revision was simply unsystematic, piecemeal, occasional—the muddles, then as now, go by so quickly on stage that they pose problems mainly for editors and readers. Those problems were not what the actor-revisers (who may or may not have included Shakespeare) were concerned with. There is a good deal in the texts of most plays of the period that even the original audience must have missed.

The revisers do seem to have been concerned with pacing, which probably explains the cutting of Lear's mock-trial of Goneril and Regan in 3.6, a favourite episode of modern directors. It is usually returned to the script now (modern productions are also usually too long). It *is* a good bit, but it holds up the action; and for plays that had to be performed in two or three hours, it must have seemed expendable—what would you cut? For us, the answer would be as much of the fool as possible: his jokes are now unfunny, and their point is often unrecoverable. But he was precisely what would not have been cut in 1623; indeed, the folio's principal addition to the quarto is the fool's fifteen-line prophecy at the end of 3.2, epigrammatically predicting a future identical to the present. About half this passage now requires glosses to make sense. If such moments work at all for us, it is not through the text but through the actor's body language. For us, the fool is a marginal figure who gives a performance largely independent of the script.

The fool in Shakespeare's theatre, however, was not marginal, but essential, the figure in whom the whole idea of performance itself was embodied, and the fact that his role was often unscripted only emphasizes the extent to which early modern drama was as much performative as textual. There is a delightfully indicative stage direction in an anonymous play called *The Tryall of Chevalrie* (1605) that reads, '*Exit clown, speaking anything*'.[6] *King Lear* is the Shakespeare play in which the fool is most deeply germane to the action, Lear's zany conscience, Cordelia's antic alter ego. Why do we still keep the fool at all? He cannot simply be cut without radically altering the play (as Tate did, and duly cut the fool); but he could be made wise and witty, or at least funny, again—this is a case where sticking to the text really does violate the spirit of the role, which has always been improvisation. Suppose you cast an actor like Zero Mostel or Amy Schumer in the role, with instructions to do whatever he or she wanted? The fool's speeches are scripted, but it is not clear that they always were, and if Robert Armin, the principal clown of The King's Men, was the original fool, he would surely have been significantly involved in the development of the role.

The folio text is still much too long to have been a performing version, but it gives a sense of how the performers worked, what sorts of things could go and what needed to be expanded—not, on the whole, the things we cut, and certainly not those we expand (for example, on the one hand, pageantry, and on the other, things that clarify the plot). There is one entirely logical revision in the folio text (in contrast to what we might call all the folio's performance-based revisions), the omission from the folio of the quarto's 4.3, with Kent's account of Lear being too ashamed to see Cordelia; this is an editorial revision. The scene is obviously part of an earlier idea about the play. There is no sign that Lear has been avoiding Cordelia when he finally does see her in 4.7, and indeed, no indication that he knows she is in England at all: the two scenes contradict each other. This sort of editorial logic is very rare in the folio's alterations.

But now consider an illogical revision: only the quarto, in 5.3, includes Edgar's account to Albany of meeting the disguised Kent just after the death of Gloucester, and of Kent revealing himself (1608: 5.3.204–18). Why would the folio cut this? Without it, Kent is never identified to Albany as Lear's mysterious retainer Caius; so that when Kent appears in the folio's play ten lines later, the only enlightenment Albany gets is Edgar's 'Here comes Kent' (1623: 5.3.205). Kent, as far as Albany knows, has been missing since the first scene and has had nothing to do with the subsequent action, and nothing explains his presence in the final scene. The folio produces a loose end that seems to have been deliberately untied. In fact, Kent never gets any kind of dramatic recognition at the end, in either version: he has come for a grand reconciliation with Lear, but he has to point out what everyone else has forgotten, that Lear is not even present. Lear himself never makes the connection between Kent and Caius. This was doubtless retained in the folio because it adds significantly to the pathos and abjectness of Lear's condition, but why then deliberately change the text to keep Albany in the dark too? Surely the irony and pathos are strongest if everyone knows Kent's double identity except Lear.

One might say that Albany does not need to know it; it is sufficient for the audience to know it, and it contributes to a kind of terminal vagueness. In contrast, however, the play also concludes with some compulsive tidying up: instead of relying simply on dramatic action, incriminating documents are produced, things that prove Goneril's villainy and Edmund's treachery, as if these were in question. For whom does evidence have to be produced? To whom is Edgar's chivalric victory and Edmund's confession insufficient to justify the treatment of the villains? Moreover, the evidence is just the kind that Edmund had initially used to impeach Edgar with—why is a letter purporting to be from Goneril any more trustworthy than a letter purporting to be from Edgar? Letters delivered by villains are inherently problematic; that is, it is not the document but the moral status of its bearer that constitutes the proof (so much for documentary evidence!). But why is a letter necessary at all? Clearly in this case it is not enough for the audience to see the justice of Edgar's charges: Albany on stage must see it. But then why remove the lines that explain Kent's presence to Albany? The compulsive elucidation leaves many holes in the plot, even more in the folio text than in the quarto.

Revising, for modern writers, is a process of tidying up, but gaps and obscurities are not the things the folio's revisers wanted to deal with. In fact, the only significant thing in the plot that was altered is the removal of references to the French king and his army from Cordelia's reappearance to rescue her father. In 3.1, the quarto says

> From France there comes a power
> Into this scattered kingdom
>
> (1608: 3.1.22–3)

which is revised to say merely that Albany and Cornwall have spies for the French among their servants. Similarly, Gloucester tells Edmund in the quarto that 'there's part of a power already landed' to avenge the king (3.3.12–13), whereas in the folio the power is 'already footed': the quarto's army comes from abroad, the folio's is domestic. But even this is not consistent: in 3.7.2–3, in both texts, 'The army of France is landed', though only the quarto has Kent and a gentleman in a later scene discussing details of the French military arrangements, with the king returning to France (1608: 4.3a.4). The change is generally explained as involving a political issue, but why should a French army on English soil be less politically sensitive in 1608 than later? In any case, Cordelia's presence must certainly constitute a French invasion. The folio merely softens the blow by removing the reference to the French king, so that the French troops become Cordelia's.[7] The revision, however, also seems to make her abandon the King of France to take charge of her father—her husband is effectively removed. In the folio, then, ironically, Cordelia does exactly what in the opening scene she swears she will never do, 'marry like my sisters/ To love my father all' (1.1.103–4). But maybe this is the point; maybe the folio wants Cordelia's reappearance to be sentimental rather than military.

Now consider a scene that neither the folio nor Tate cut, and that, until well into the nineteenth century was both widely deplored and considered indispensable, the blinding of Gloucester. Samuel Johnson wrote of this 'that the cruelty of the daughters is an historical fact, . . . But I am not able to apologise with equal plausibility for the extrusion of Gloucester's eyes, which seems an act too horrid to be endured in dramatick exhibition, and such as must always compel the mind to relieve its distress by incredulity.'[8] But Johnson continues with a strikingly relativistic apology for the scene: 'Yet let it be remembered that our authour well knew what would please the audience for which he wrote.' This begs some questions (the scene was still being played for the audiences of Johnson's time, and for decades thereafter) but Johnson's strategy here, to focus not on the stage, but on the audience, and on the audience, moreover, as an impediment to revision, is one I wish to pursue.

The blinding scene is in its way unique not only in Shakespearean drama, but in the drama of the period. Hypocritical speeches, forged letters, sending elderly fathers out in the rain, not having respect for kingship, conning one's brother out of his inheritance, are all fairly unsurprising indices to villainy in Renaissance drama. How much more villainous do the villains have to be in *King Lear*? The villains' badness is literalized through torture and mutilation; but though the play often works by actualizing its metaphors—Lear's rage becoming the storm, Gloucester describing Regan's cruelty as plucking out Lear's eyes—one of the reasons the scene is so shocking is precisely the fact of how unprepared we are for it.

The scene's dramatic intensity is so powerful that it prompts a critical tendency to dissipate it, for example, by allegorizing it (it realizes Gloucester's moral blindness), and in fact the play does some of that as well: Gloucester himself later says 'I have no way and therefore want no eyes/ I stumbled when I saw' (4.1.18–19), and his response to the terrible taunt 'Out vile jelly/ Where is thy lustre now?' is 'All dark and comfortless' (3.7.84–5), which is really impossible to say in a realistic performance—instead of a howl of pain, the actor is required to produce a brief, elegiac parallel with the comfortless Lear in the storm. In the theatre, however, we are confronted not with textual parallels, but with violent and painful action presented directly on stage. Giorgio Strehler's 1972 production turned the scene into a very kinky sexual game between Cornwall and Regan in black leather, with Gloucester invisible in the trap beneath. This has a point, in the sense that the scene is really establishing something about Cornwall and Regan, not about Gloucester—we know all the ways in which Gloucester is blind; what we do not know is the full force of evil realizing itself in the play. But real evil produces real blindness, and that might be a reason for keeping Gloucester onstage, forcing the scene on our eyesight.

Still, this does not quite describe what occurs dramatically, because after all, nothing really happens to Gloucester: this is a play. But if we withdraw from the scene in this way—Gloucester is a fictional character impersonated by various actors over and over, none of whom ever gets blinded—we are all the more aware that what happens in the scene happens not to the character but to the audience; and if we consider the scene in this light, it is not at all unique: there are many other comparable scenes. Elizabethan pamphlets are full of explicit accounts of horrible tortures inflicted on prisoners; and executions, sometimes involving drawing and quartering or burning alive, were a species of popular entertainment. John Foxe's book of martyrs *Actes and Monuments*, with its ghastly accounts of the sufferings of Protestant heroes, adorned with ghastly woodcuts, was a continual best seller throughout the age, not only for its devotional matter; the devotional and the lurid are clearly aspects of each other. It may be that tastes have changed somewhat in this respect, though they certainly have not changed so much that we cannot see the point—S&M is, after all, still very much in fashion, and sadism is increasingly a staple of popular movies. Maybe the point of this scene is just the opposite of the one we try to get out of it: we are horrified at the treatment of the good people by the bad people, outraged by the villainy of the villainous, but suddenly here is a scene that puts us firmly in collusion with the villains—this is the scene that gives Shakespeare's audience what they really like, the pleasures of torture and mutilation with a good moral context to boot. 'Let it be remembered', says the judicious Johnson, 'that our authour well knew what would please the audience for which he wrote.'

So how bad are Cornwall and Regan? Just about as bad as we are; they are doing it for our pleasure. The folio makes just one revision to the scene, deleting the pitying and moralizing servants. That seems designed to emphasize our complicity, to keep us focused on the theatre of cruelty, to avoid introducing a surrogate pity that detaches us from the action. The scene, moreover, cannot be accounted for as an indication of the savagery of early modern taste: although commentators have been universally appalled by it, few revisers, and none till the mid-nineteenth century, found a way of doing without it. Tate says he could not think of a way of cutting it and maintaining the plot. Whatever else it is, it has seemed both structurally essential and a necessary principle of explanation. Still, it is hard to see the resistance to moving the blinding itself offstage as anything but disingenuous. The scene is simply too powerful a piece of theatre for the performing tradition to abandon it.

The first recorded performance of *King Lear* is the one cited on the 1608 quarto title page, at court before King James, on Dec 26, 1606. There is no other known performance in London or at court before the Restoration; the only other early record is one I have already discussed (in Chapter 1), a private performance given by a provincial company in a gentleman's house in Yorkshire—a group of Catholic players were indicted in 1610 for performing Catholic propaganda there. They defended themselves by arguing that their performing texts were the published quartos, which had been duly licensed. This was not an adequate defence because the licensing of books is a different matter from the licensing of plays; but even more because the relation between the text of a play and the staged script is quite simply imponderable. This is why the licensing of plays included a specific injunction that no more was allowed to be spoken than appeared in the script, a stipulation that was as essential as it was unenforceable—it was the violation of this principle that was chiefly at issue here. The most significant part of this story for modern assumptions about early playtexts is the testimony that the first quartos of *King Lear* and *Pericles*, which are both, for us, hornets' nests of editorial problems, were the bases for perfectly usable theatrical scripts in the period.[9]

The paucity of the stage history of *King Lear* is odd for so widely cited a play, and presumably means that we have lost the records, not that there were no performances. It was republished in quarto in 1655, when the theatres were closed; so there was still a market for it, and when the theatres reopened in 1660, it was frequently performed, first in the folio version, and then, ubiquitously, in Tate's revision, to which I now turn.

The happy ending is the most notorious of Tate's changes to the plot, though in a way it is the least surprising. As I have indicated, in every other version of the Lear story, both in the chronicles and in the earlier play on the subject called *The True Chronicle History of King Leir*, Lear's throne is restored to him, he dies in peace, and in some sources Cordelia rules after him. She is subsequently deposed, imprisoned, and commits suicide, but that is part of another story; she has heirs, and both the continuity of Lear's line and the facts of early British history are assured. In those sources where she survives,

Cordelia is succeeded by Goneril's son, which is ironic; but Edgar, on whom Shakespeare bestows the kingdom, has no place in the line of succession at all, and is a fictional character anyway. To kill off both Lear and Cordelia and give the kingdom to Edgar was both historically perverse and a significant defeat for any early audience's expectations. It is not even clear in Shakespeare why Edgar should be promoted to the throne at all, to say nothing of Kent, whom Albany designates as co-ruler with Edgar, though Kent declines the honour.

Of the characters left alive, Albany himself would seem to have the best claim to succeed Lear, being both his son-in-law and the victor in the battle for the kingdom; but instead he ends the play by dividing up the kingdom again, this time between two people who have no claim to it. Is there really nothing here for critical commentary to take account of? Shakespeare is not especially faithful to history elsewhere, but this is surely an extreme example, analogous to making Henry V lose the battle of Agincourt, and installing somebody—anybody—else as king. From Tate to Johnson, a standard element in the defence of the happy ending was that it was true. It was Shakespeare who had changed the ending, not Tate. For Shakespeare's original audiences, the ending of the play was a surprise.

The question of why (and how) Shakespeare changed the ending has not been a serious one for us. Tate's ending, we argue, trivializes the suffering, though the subtext of this argument is surely that if Shakespeare did it, it must be right. But there is nothing normative, even within Shakespeare's own work, that dictated the tragic ending. What he added to a very mixed plot was a degree of abjectness and cruelty unmatched in his drama since *Titus Andronicus*. It is precisely those elements that we do not take seriously. Johnson takes them seriously, when he says that 'I was many years ago so shocked by Cordelia's death, that I know not whether I ever endured to read again the last scenes of the play till I undertook to revise them as an editor.'[10] Surely it is worth asking what seemed to require an outcome at once so bleak and so unexpected, in a dramaturgy that could produce tragicomedy like *Measure for Measure, Cymbeline, Pericles, The Winter's Tale*, all plays whose sufferings are redeemed in a reversal of fortune that we might even call characteristically Shakespearean.

The answer to this question may well be biographical, and therefore beyond the limits of our evidence. Nevertheless, it is worth recognizing as an issue, and insisting that the ending is not one that is determined by the plot. This is a play in which Shakespeare goes out of his way to raise expectations only to (perhaps in order to) defeat them. Cordelia's aborted survival is not the only one. What about the recognition of Edgar by the blind Gloucester, which is reported in a single line as an afterthought in *King Lear*, but is where Shakespeare's source story in Sidney's *Arcadia* starts, the perspective from which the whole story is told by the reconciled father and son? In Shakespeare, on the contrary, it is precisely the revelation of Edgar's identity that kills Gloucester.

Perhaps, however, we judge the general tone of the play, its exceptional bleakness, by an anachronistic standard. For us, Lear starts out with an obvious display of temperament, which unleashes all the problems. Notice, however, that though it is Kent who initially objects to Lear's bad judgment, only the villains believe that it renders him unfit to rule. In fact, elsewhere he is referred to in the play not as blind, foolish, irascible, self-centred, mad, incompetent (or as we would sum it up, senile), but as *kind*—Kent says 'the hard rein which both of them have borne/ Against the old kind king...' (1623: 3.1.19–20). Lear on himself, 'So kind a father!' (1.5.32), is presumably to be taken ironically, but later, 'Your old kind father, whose frank heart gave all' (1608: 3.4.19–20; 1623: 3.4.20), is, objectively, accurate. When Richard Burbage, Shakespeare's leading man, died in 1619, his elegy lists the roles that made him famous:

> young Hamlet, old Hieronymo [in *The Spanish Tragedy*]
> kind Lear, the grievèd Moor [Othello]....[11]

Kind Lear. All these examples insist on Lear's essential goodness. For a Jacobean audience, however, the largest point would surely be that even a bad king is still the king. This is no doubt why King James liked this play about a monarch destroyed by his heirs enough to have it performed for him at court. For us, Shakespeare's play is about the responsibilities of kingship; how thoughtless small acts can have incalculably terrible effects; how little we understand even the people who are closest to us; above all, about our capacity for suffering, and about the fact that however bad things are, they can always be worse. But Shakespeare's surprise ending also impressed on Jacobean audiences that ignoring the patriarchal imperatives not only brought chaos to the kingdom, but destroyed the line of succession, and indeed, overturned history itself. So perhaps our objections to the sentimentalization of the play that Tate's version represents are anachronistic. It was already quite a sentimental play; we have adopted the point of view of the villains. Tate's version is sentimental in a different way, but he does understand something about the play in Shakespeare's time that we have forgotten.

Many of Tate's revisions were dictated by contemporary political issues, but there are other considerations as well. There was the necessity for increasing the scope of the female roles for a theatre in which women were now significant players. The basic question, however, is not what happens when women are played by women rather than by young men, but what differences the culture assumes between men and women, and what constitutes an acceptable representation of either. The issue here obviously has to do not with sex, but with gender—not with chromosomes and genital organs, but with codes of behaviour.

In one respect, all the trouble is caused by Cordelia's initial refusal to give a performance. But good women in Shakespeare's society are supposed to be silent. Cordelia starts by playing the traditional female role, one that women are praised for, and that women in Shakespeare generally do not play. It is Lear who violates the traditional gender codes by forcing his daughters, especially the unmarried one, to speak. It is important to emphasize, however, that in this case the cultural norm is never a Shakespearean norm: think of Shakespeare's heroines, Portia, Rosalind, Beatrice, Juliet. A counter-example such as the silent Virgilia in *Coriolanus* (her husband refers to her as 'my gracious silence'), is balanced in *Coriolanus* by Coriolanus's mother, the voluble Volumnia. In general, however, the issue of female volubility in Shakespeare is more conventional than gendered: in comedy, the female speakers are unmarried, and good fun; in tragedy, they are married, and disruptive, or even absolutely villainous: the murderous bullying of Lady Macbeth is reprehensible, but so, in *The Winter's Tale*, is the shrewish Paulina's entirely virtuous refusal to obey her husband and the king and be silent. As a cultural assumption, for wives to talk is much more dangerous than for unmarried women to do so: women eventually pass from their fathers' control, but not from their husbands'. It must be to the point that the fathers of Portia, Viola, Olivia, Beatrice, Helena, Isabella, are all dead; and Rosalind's father, though alive, is effectively silenced, and is given no say in his daughter's marriage arrangements.

The gender imperatives in *King Lear* actually seem less significant than the patriarchal imperatives, nor are these uniform: the patriarchy of fathers often conflicts with that of husbands. In fact, the position of husbands and fathers in the play is arguably more to the point than the position of women; husbands and fathers are the endangered species. Questions of inheritance, the basic patriarchal questions, are the key ones: Lear dividing his property in three is following Elizabethan law, by which, while sons inherit according to primogeniture (the eldest gets everything), daughters inherit equally. Legally, Lear's division of the kingdom is at fault only in attempting to give Cordelia a better share than her sisters. The problems of primogeniture are the subject of the Gloucester plot, where Edmund is doubly disadvantaged: he is not only illegitimate, he is the younger son as well. Even if he were legitimate he still would be entitled to nothing. The issue in all these cases has to do not with the position of sons as opposed to daughters, but with the position of children in relation to their fathers and to each other.

What then does gender have to do with it? It is the focus of the erotics of the play, certainly, though these also have little to do with the issues of marriage that fill the opening scene—'tell me how much you love me' is what fathers say to children in *King Lear*, not what lovers say to each other. As for the erotics of the opening scene, Burgundy and France have come to woo Cordelia, but for both, the primary issue is inheritance, not love. There is absolutely nothing culturally inappropriate about this: the reason women in this culture are provided with dowries is that men will not marry them otherwise. Women are property, and the more property they represent the more desirable they are.

So why does Cordelia become more attractive to the king of France when she is dowryless, and out of favour with the king? This is the romance element in the plot; the love interest suddenly materializes, and is represented as entirely quixotic. Of course, France's romantic passion can also be seen realistically (or cynically) as representing basically an investment. France supporting an invasion of England by an army led by his wife is hardly disinterested; France is not concerned solely to get Lear in out of the rain. To rescue Lear is to repossess Cordelia's third of the kingdom, and perhaps much more. Cordelia is a gamble, but in the sources the gamble pays off handsomely— Cordelia becomes queen. The surprise for a Jacobean audience would have been that in Shakespeare it does not pay off.

Where then are the erotics of the play? They are in the villains, the adulterous passion of Goneril and Regan for Edmund, which turns the sisters from natural allies to natural enemies. In Shakespeare's version, this has much more to do with plotting and villainy than with passion: we hear about the sisters' pursuit of Edmund, and Edmund admits that he has courted both, but there are no love scenes. Edmund is sometimes played as glamorous and sexually magnetic; that works very well, but it really is adding a dimension to the play that is scarcely suggested. The love affairs in the text are all basically just more intrigue: the lust on Edmund's side is for power; and as for the sisters, so far as we can tell, they kill each other off before any sex happens. Gloucester's past adultery casts an increasingly ominous shadow, but is there any evidence of adultery taking place in the play's present tense? The lust and passion consist, dramatically at least, of writing letters, which ultimately get revealed to the one surviving husband. The adultery is literally textual.

Tate's most significant alteration to Shakespeare's plot comes not at the end but at the beginning: Cordelia and Edgar are in love. This is Tate's way of accounting for Cordelia's behaviour in the opening scene: her refusal to play Lear's game is strategic, preventing her from being married off to Burgundy (France has been entirely eliminated). As a dramatic device, the romance has come under attack since the eighteenth century; and it does certainly neaten and rationalize the plot. But in fact Cordelia's behaviour in the opening scene has always been a problem—is she culpable or not? Surely the issue at the outset was not simply honest silence versus lying rhetoric, but involved both a violation of courtesy and an insensitivity to the infirmity of her father's condition and the complexity of his nature. If Lear throws away Cordelia's love, so does Cordelia throw away Lear's. One may not want this issue settled, or sidestepped, so neatly, but criticism has on the whole idealized Cordelia in this scene, and Tate confronts a question that commentators have preferred to avoid.

If love is a principle of explanation in Tate's *King Lear*, lust is a principle of politics—Tate brings into the open things that are implied or alluded to in Shakespeare, but seem to be underplayed; and in the Restoration revision a careful balance of the erotic and the political is maintained. The most spectacular scene in Tate is the attempted rape of Cordelia by Edmund: sex is a destructive weapon, a way of getting revenge and exerting control. (She is rescued, of course, by Edgar.) Tate's Edmund begins his ascent by announcing his passion for 'the proud imperial sisters'.[12] Gloucester's rebellious support of Lear is explicit and forceful: Cordelia, who is present throughout the action, enlists his aid, and he replies that 'I have already plotted to restore/ My injured master' (pp. 23–4). They are overheard by Edmund, who declares his passion for Cordelia and his intention of betraying his father in the same speech. He says he will kidnap Cordelia, and then rape her as the wind and thunder drown out her cries. The attack on Cordelia and her rescue by Edgar was one of the great set-pieces of Tate's play. The scene concludes with Cordelia and Edgar declaring and confirming their love.

The blinding scene follows this. Tate speeds it up and lingers less than Shakespeare over the sadism. He also, characteristically, adds an erotic twist: as Edmund is sent away in deference to his filial feelings, he is propositioned by Regan, and goes off to await her in a grotto. The blinded Gloucester, thrust out of doors, determines to remain a political force:

> I will present me to the pitying crowd,
> And with the rhetoric of these dropping veins
> Enflame 'em to revenge their king and me.
>
> (p. 33)

Exactly what Goneril and Regan fear in Shakespeare comes to pass in Tate. Regan and Edmund's love scene in the grotto immediately follows.

The Dover Cliff scene is retained, but Tate frames it with scenes of the growing rebellion. The revived Gloucester persuades Kent to lead the troops, and a Cordelia who by this time has little in common with Shakespeare's heroine ends Act 4 with a warlike speech. After this, the play moves to its conclusion with a mass of plotting. Goneril orders poison to be prepared for Regan; Edmund plans a move from Regan, with whom he has already slept, to Goneril, whom he has yet to possess:

> Cornwall is dead, and Regan's empty bed
> Seems cast by fortune for me, but already
> I have enjoyed her, and bright Goneril
> With equal charms brings dear variety,
> And yet untasted beauty. . . .
>
> (p. 46)

Tate's Edmund speaks with the erotic sensibility of a Restoration rake, but the underlying sexual politics are Shakespeare's.

At the end, where Shakespeare's Albany gives the kingdom to Kent and Edgar, Tate's Albany gives it to Cordelia and Edgar. The marriage Tate invents for them in one sense subverts Shakespeare's conclusion, but in another sense vindicates it: the only way for Edgar to succeed to the throne is as Cordelia's husband. Tate's *King Lear* is sentimental and melodramatic; it is also clear, well paced, dramatically effective, and as its long presence in the theatre confirms, eminently stageable. From a modern perspective, it is most interesting as a critical reading of Shakespeare, confronting genuine problems in the play. We have, on the whole, preferred to deal with these through elucidation and commentary, rather than through theatrical revision—we tend now to prefer bibliographical explanations (and revisions) to narrative ones; but what that does is move the play increasingly away from the stage and toward the book and the putative manuscript behind it.

6

Pericles Prince of Tyre

Pericles was one of Shakespeare's most popular plays, both among readers and audiences. It appeared in six quarto editions by 1635 (surpassed only by the perennial favourites *Richard III* and 1 *Henry IV*; *Richard III* by 1634 had appeared in eight quartos, 1 *Henry IV* by 1639 in nine—for comparison, the two versions of Marlowe's *Doctor Faustus* appeared in eight quarto editions between 1604 and 1631, *The Spanish Tragedy* in twelve by 1633). It was the first Shakespeare play produced after the reopening of the theatres in 1660, with Thomas Betterton in the title role. For Ben Jonson, the popularity of *Pericles* in the theatre became a touchstone for the vulgarity of contemporary taste. Resolving to abandon the stage after the failure of his play *The New Inne*, Jonson deplored audiences' admiration for 'a mouldy tale/ Like *Pericles*'.[1] The play was not included in the first folio in 1623, possibly because it was a collaboration (the many textual problems of the quarto would not have been an obstacle, since the editors would have had access to the King's Men's prompt-book), but probably simply because the quartos were selling well—there had been one in 1619, and would be another in 1630—and doubtless the rights to reprint the play could not be obtained.

It was finally included in the third and fourth folios (1664 and 1685), along with six other plays that had been credited to Shakespeare in his lifetime. The seven plays continued to be integral to Shakespeare's works until Pope's edition of 1721, from which they were banished, though they were subsequently included in Pope's second edition of 1728 (this was a decision of the publisher, not of Pope). The seven plays then definitively disappeared from Shakespeare's works until

1780, when Edmond Malone, the editor who did more to establish our notion of what constitutes Shakespeare than anyone since the editors of the first folio, ascribed *Pericles*, but not the other six plays, to Shakespeare in the George Steevens and Samuel Johnson edition of Shakespeare's works.[2] The play has since that time retained a firm if anomalous place in the Shakespeare canon, while the other plays from the third folio have become the 'Shakespeare apocrypha'.

The earliest reference to the play is an entry in the Stationers' Register on 20 May, 1608, by the publisher Edward Blount. On the same day Blount also registered *Antony and Cleopatra*. But Blount did not go on to publish either play. The quarto of *Pericles* that appeared in 1609, published by Henry Gosson, does not relate to this entry: Blount would have had to transfer his rights in the book to Gosson, and did not do so, and there is no new entry for Gosson's book. This was irregular, but not illegal. Much of what Gosson printed was ephemera, and he had never printed a play; but he was not a piratical publisher, and he may simply have been avoiding the registration fee. A fair number of books published in the period have no Stationers' Register entries, and nothing about Gosson's quarto suggests that it was surreptitious. The failure to register the book would have caused trouble only if Blount had decided subsequently to exercise his right. It does imply, however, that the text Gosson published was different from the text Blount had entered—that is, that Gosson had some text other than the one that would have been provided by the performers.

What Gosson's copy was it is difficult to say. The text is very muddled. Editors long believed that its confusions and obvious errors indicated a memorial reconstruction of some sort, but more recent commentators have argued that similarities with the text of the 1608 quarto of *King Lear* suggest that it derives at least in part from an authorial rough draft. Clearly the printers had difficulty reading their copy, and from the second quarto onward editors have found it necessary to emend merely to make sense of the text. None of the editions after the first depends on an independent text—this is a 'bad quarto' where we have no good text to compare it with. The actual production of the book was a complex collaboration. As Gary Taylor and MacDonald Jackson in their textual introduction to the play observe, 'The division of work on Q between (certainly) two printers and (probably) three compositors provides the strongest possible evidence that the deficiencies of the text—present in the work of both printers—originate in the manuscript copy, not in the process of printing.'[3]

The play, then, offers a good index to what, historically, has been seen as authentically Shakespearean. There are undeniably wonderful things in *Pericles*, but excellence has rarely been the crucial test. Another of the apocryphal plays, *The Yorkshire Tragedy*, has long been recognized as a powerful and original Elizabethan drama. To our ears it does not sound much like Shakespeare, but the sound of Shakespeare is not really the test. As we have observed (in Chapter 2), *King John* and *The Merry Wives of Windsor* do not sound like each other, and neither sounds any more Shakespearean than *The Yorkshire Tragedy*; and *Titus Andronicus* has sounded so little like Shakespeare that it was declared spurious by many critics from the eighteenth to the mid-twentieth century. Nevertheless, it remained in the canon. The first and second parts of Shakespeare's early history play *Henry VI* provide a different kind of example: they are clearly collaborations, yet throughout their editorial history they have remained 'Shakespeare'. And Shakespeare's final history play *Henry VIII* has for the past century and a half been assumed to be a collaboration with John Fletcher, though there is no evidence to support this view except the fact that there are sections of it that do not sound like Shakespeare—or do not sound like what we want Shakespeare to sound like: the sound of Shakespeare has varied widely from age to age.

Why did Malone declare *Pericles* authentic, then, and not *The Yorkshire Tragedy* or the rest of the apocrypha? There is no answer to this question outside the play itself: there is something in it we want to claim for Shakespeare, something our Shakespeare cannot do without. There were from the beginning, however, problems about introducing it into the canon. The 1609 quarto, as we have seen, presents numerous textual difficulties. The first two acts are stylistically so different from the rest of the play that they seem to be the work of someone else; many passages throughout the play are incoherent, and much that is obviously verse has been printed as prose. Nevertheless, this was not a surreptitious or pirated edition; the King's Men did not subsequently publish a 'correct' version of the play, and indeed, at a time when Shakespeare's company was taking systematic legal action to protect its literary property, they ignored *Pericles*, and the 1609 quarto was reprinted five times before 1635. The play, both on the stage and in print, was hugely popular; it was one of Shakespeare's most popular and widely performed plays, yet the King's Men never asserted their right to it—as far as publication was concerned, they did not own it. And problematic as the quarto is, it is in fact no more problematic than several other Shakespeare quartos, and differs from them only in that there is no subsequent 'good' text.

The quarto text, then, is the only text. When the editors of the third folio included the play in Shakespeare's works in 1664, they had no choice but to reprint the quarto once again. Problematic as it seems to us—and it undeniably presents insurmountable difficulties for a modern editor—in Shakespeare's age it was in most respects a satisfactory text. I have already cited (in Chapter 1) the 1610 Yorkshire players who derived their performing script from it, as Betterton in his 1660 production must have done. Much of the difficulty that editors have had with *Pericles* has to do with its failure to read like the edited texts of the folio. But its unedited look has much in common with the first quartos of *Hamlet* and *Romeo and Juliet*, and its often baffling textual problems are similar to those of the first quarto of *King Lear*, which, for all its confusions, seems to derive from

Shakespeare's original draft of the play. To turn it into a normative reading text would be to emend that archaeology out of it, which would be possible, in any case, only by rewriting it.

The play's textual confusion does not end with the quarto. There is also a prose version of the story apparently based on the play. The title page of George Wilkins's *The Painfull Adventures of Pericles Prince of Tyre*, published in 1608, a year before the first quarto of *Pericles*, declares that it is 'the true history of the play of *Pericles*, as it was lately presented by the worthy and ancient poet John Gower'. Wilkins's narrative does indeed generally follow the action of the play (though Gower appears nowhere in it after the title page), and gives fuller, or at least rationalized, versions of a number of problematic incidents. However, Wilkins's novel also relies heavily on an earlier version of the Pericles story which had in turn served as a source for the play, Lawrence Twine's translation of a French romance about the life of a hero named Apollonius of Tyre, *The Patterne of Painefull Adventures*, published in 1594. And Gower's *Confessio Amantis* also has a version of the story. The relation between Wilkins's novel and the play, therefore, is by no means straightforward.

Similarities in vocabulary and syntax between the play and Wilkins's novel at critical points make it arguable that if the play is a collaboration, Wilkins was Shakespeare's collaborator. Commentators have resisted the suggestion because Wilkins was a writer of little distinction and a thoroughly bad character (though he was the author of a popular play called *The Miseries of Inforst Marriage*), and they do not like the idea of Shakespeare collaborating with a hack and a scoundrel; but the idea is not inconsistent with what we know about the business of theatre in Shakespeare's time. The fact that the only Shakespearean collaborator whose name we know is the very distinguished playwright John Fletcher may certainly imply that Shakespeare did not stoop to collaborating with hacks; but it may equally mean only that we do not know much about Shakespeare's collaborators (to say nothing of his feelings about them), since the folio does not acknowledge collaborations. Not only the first two *Henry VI* plays but also *Macbeth* have demonstrably non-Shakespearean elements, yet in the folio they are all Shakespeare; whereas the one play we know he wrote with Fletcher, *The Two Noble Kinsmen*, was not included in the volume. (I see no reason to assume that Shakespeare had anything to do with the ghostly *Cardenio*.)[4] And of course it is also quite possible that Shakespeare thought better of Wilkins than we do.

It is undeniable that the first two acts of *Pericles* are radically different in style from the rest of the play. Critics who want to insist that the play is all by Shakespeare, as F. D. Hoeniger in the 1963 Arden 2 edition and, though more cautiously, Doreen DelVecchio and Antony Hammond in the 1998 New Cambridge edition do, have to assume that the first two acts have suffered egregiously in transmission, even more egregiously than the last three, which also have serious problems—though, as Suzanne Gossett points out in the excellent Arden 3 edition, the first two acts are in fact more satisfactorily printed in the first quarto than the rest of the play, which suggests a more satisfactory manuscript.[5] DelVecchio and Hammond conclude by concurring with the 1987 New Oxford editors that the play is a masterpiece, and therefore declare the question of who wrote it 'interesting but fundamentally irrelevant'. I too like the play, but the question of authorship is surely not irrelevant at all, if the whole point is to include the play in a complete Shakespeare. It is doubtless the case that in its own time the play did enjoy its immense popularity because it was a masterpiece—or at least that, by the standards of the Renaissance stage, it was very good theatre. This is not, however, an argument in its favour now; other blockbusters of the Renaissance stage, such as the perennially popular anonymous *Mucedorus* or Thomas Middleton's notorious *A Game at Chesse*, survive only, barely, in scholarly editions, and there are many very good Renaissance plays—very good even by modern standards—that are rarely read and never performed. The excellence of *Pericles* is not in question, but its excellence is precisely what is fundamentally irrelevant. The play excites whatever interest it enjoys today only because Shakespeare's name is attached to it.

Once we have settled on the date, 1608, the play becomes 'late', and 'late Shakespeare' for us implies a calm and wise playwright, Shakespeare after all that turbulent drama arriving at acceptance and reconciliation. If *Pericles* is to be the gateway to Shakespearean romance, there are still things we need to rescue the play from. The brothel scenes have been a major stumbling block, and constitute the principal argument for Wilkins's continuing involvement in the play's composition after the first two acts. Lucy Munro gives a deadpan but quite funny account of the RSC's attempts to sanitize the behaviour in the brothel of Lysimachus, the disguised governor of Mytilene, and strengthen Miranda's behaviour, for a Terry Hands production in 1969.[6] Certainly as the text reads, Lysimachus behaves badly, though it is not clear how reprehensible he would have been found in 1608—for comparison, in Sidney's *Arcadia*, the pastoral romance of the noble hero Mucidorus and the virtuous heroine Pamela includes an attempted rape, but Mucidorus continues to be a hero. Modern editors and directors of *Pericles*, however, import material from Wilkins's *Painful Adventures* and rearrange and delete sections to make Lysimachus less debauched and Marina more vulnerable and thereby more persuasive, which is to say, more 'feminine'. Munro sees this as making the play 'late', though I would call it an attempt to make the play more acceptably modern.

It strikes me, however, as a missed opportunity. For our moment in history, there is surely an alternative way of viewing the brothel scenes. In them, Marina is not only articulate, but fully in command, both of her situation and of Lysimachus—a very Shakespearean woman, if we think of Portia, Rosalind, Lady Macbeth, Cleopatra, Paulina. After the brothel scenes, what is unclear to me in dramatic terms is why marrying Marina off to Lysimachus should constitute a satisfactory resolution, especially since Marina is given no say in the matter, not one word, even of assent—surely half a line would have been enough. This is especially striking since her mother Thaisa, earlier in the play, is so forceful about choosing her own husband: the play clearly represents this as a possible option for women. Why is it not an option for Marina? Why, indeed, would Marina want to marry Lysimachus, the frequenter of brothels in disguise? What has become of the Shakespeare of *As You Like It*—or shall we say that at this point the author of *The Miseries of Inforst Mariage* has reappeared,[7] and that the ending predicts an unhappy future for Marina?

7

Macbeth

There is no quarto of *Macbeth*, and if there were, it would be very different from the play we know. Textually the play is an anomaly in the folio, in that it is demonstrably a revision. It includes songs for the witches, but these appear only with their opening words, that is, as references to another text: 'Come away, come away, etc.'; 'Black spirits, etc.' These songs come from Thomas Middleton's play *The Witch*. In performance they were accompanied by dances, which means that in the theatre these scenes took much longer than they do on the page. Sir William Davenant's revision of *Macbeth*, prepared around 1664, includes the whole text of the witches' songs from Middleton—these are really musical dialogues, short scenes. Davenant provided his own witches' material elsewhere, and this suggests that the Middleton material was already part of the play. *The Witch* was not printed until the late eighteenth century, and therefore the Middleton material was presumably in the King's Men's manuscript of the play.

The elaboration of the witches' roles could have taken place anywhere up to about fifteen years after the play was first performed, but the presence of the Middleton songs suggests that Shakespeare was no longer present to do the revising, which presumes a date after 1614. Why, only a decade after the play was written, would augmenting the witches' roles have seemed a good idea? To begin with, by 1610 or so witchcraft, magic, and the diabolical were good theatre business— Barnabe Barnes's *The Devil's Charter* was at the Globe in the same season as *Macbeth*, and John Marston's *The Wonder of Women*, with its sorcery scenes, was at the Blackfriars. Ben Jonson's *Masque of Queens*, performed at court in 1609, inaugurated a decade of sorcery plays and masques, including *The Tempest, The Alchemist, The Witch, The Witch of Edmonton, The Devil is an Ass*, and the revived and rewritten *Doctor Faustus*.

And of course, *Macbeth*. But in *Macbeth* the witches do more than entertain the theatre audience. When Macbeth goes to consult them after the murder of Banquo, they summon up a vision of Banquo's heirs culminating in King James, which terrifies Macbeth. Hecate proposes a little cheering entertainment:

> I'll charm the air to give a sound
> While you perform your antic round,
> That this great king may kindly say
> Our duties did his welcome pay.
>
> (4.1.145–8)

The witches suddenly become gracious and deferential. It has been plausibly suggested that the 'great king' here is not the king on stage, but instead a real king in the audience, Banquo's descendant and the king of both Scotland and England.

The editors of both the Oxford and Cambridge editions have resisted the suggestion that this moment in *Macbeth* reflects the local conditions of a court performance, observing that nothing in the scene positively requires such an assumption. Nevertheless, nothing about the suggestion is implausible, and though there is no record of a court performance, King James, who made himself an expert on witchcraft, surely must have wanted to see a play that includes both witches and his ancestors. What are the implications if we assume that the text we have is a revision to take into account the presence of the king, and that his interest in witchcraft also accounts for the augmentation of the witches' scenes, so that the 'filthy, . . . black and midnight hags' become graciously entertaining after they have finished being ominously informative? The folio's *Macbeth* with its Middleton scenes is a significantly collaborative enterprise. But this version of the play also seems to be a special case, devised for a single occasion, a performance at court, not the play in repertory, the play for the public.

This assumption leads us to another question: how did this text become the standard version—why was it the right version to include in the folio? It needs to be emphasized that this is a question whether we assume that a performance before the king is involved or not: there is no denying that this is a revised text with non-Shakespearean material. Most attempts to deal with this issue beg the question, assuming that what we have is indeed the wrong text, and that Shakespeare's first editors would never have included it if they had had any alternative. The right text, the text we want (the prompt-book, or even better, Shakespeare's holograph) must have been unavailable, lost—burned, perhaps, in the destruction of the Globe in 1613, as if only a conflagration could explain the refusal of Heminges and Condell (who promise, after all, 'the true original copies') to give us what we want. But perhaps it was included precisely because it was the right text—whether because by 1620 this, quite simply, was the play, or, more interestingly, because the best version of the play was the one that included the king.

This would make it an anomaly in the folio, a version based on the play as prepared for a single, special occasion. In fact, the play as it stands in the folio is anomalous in a number of respects. It is a very unusual play textually: it is very short, the shortest of the tragedies (half the length of *Hamlet*, a third shorter than the average), shorter, too than all the comedies except *The Comedy of Errors*. It looks, moreover, as if the version we have has not only been augmented with witches' business, but has also been heavily cut: since plays at court were normally significantly longer than those in the public theatres, the augmented script could not have been what was performed on the company's usual stages, and would have had to be cut to return to the Globe. The cutting also apparently involved some rearrangement, producing real muddles in the narrative: for example, the scene between Lenox and the Lord, 3.6, reporting action that has not happened yet, or the notorious syntactic puzzles of the account of the battle in the opening scenes, or the confusion of the final battle, in which Macbeth is slain by Macduff onstage, and twenty lines later Macduff re-enters with his head. Revision and cutting were, of course, standard and necessary procedures in a theatre where the normal playing time was two or three hours; but if theatrical cuts are to explain the peculiarities of this text, why was it cut so peculiarly, not to say ineptly? Arguments that make the muddles not the result of cutting but an experiment in surreal and expressionistic dramaturgy only produce more questions, rendering the play a total anomaly, both in Shakespeare's work and in the drama of the period.

The very presence of the witches is unusual. Shakespeare makes use of the supernatural from time to time—for example, ghosts in *Richard III*, *Julius Caesar*, and most notably in *Hamlet*; fairies and their magic in *A Midsummer Night's Dream*; Prospero's sorcery in *The Tempest*; Joan of Arc's and Marjory Jourdain's in the *Henry VI* plays; and Rosalind's claim to be a magician at the end of *As You Like It*—but there is no other play in which witches and witchcraft are such an integral element of the plot. Indeed, whether or not King James was in the audience, the fact that it is the witches who provide the royal entertainment can hardly be accidental. The king was intensely interested in witchcraft; his dialogue on the subject, *Dæmonology*, first published in Edinburgh in 1597, was reissued (three times) upon his accession to the English throne in 1603. This and the *Basilicon Doron*, his philosophy of kingship, were the two works that he chose to introduce himself to his English subjects, and as I have argued elsewhere, witchcraft and kingship have an intimate relationship in the Jacobean royal ideology.[1] This is a culture in which the supernatural and witchcraft, even for sceptics, are as much part of reality as religious truth is. Like the ghost in *Hamlet*, the reality of the witches in *Macbeth* is not in question; the question, as in *Hamlet*, is why they are present and how far to believe them.

Like the ghost, too, the witches are quintessential theatrical devices: they dance and sing, perform wonders, appear and disappear, fly, produce visions—do, in short, all the things that, historically, we have gone to the theatre to see. They open the play and set the tone for it. On Shakespeare's stage they would simply have materialized through a trap door, but Shakespeare's audience believed in magic already. Our rationalistic theatre requires something quite different, generally working to remove the mystification. For Shakespeare's audience, the mystery is built into their physical appearance, which defies the categories: they look like men and are women. The indeterminacy of their gender is the first thing Banquo calls attention to. This is a defining element of their nature, a paradox that identifies them as witches: a specifically female propensity to evil—being a witch—is defined by its apparent masculinity. This also is, of course, one of the central charges levelled at Shakespeare's theatre itself, the ambiguity of its gender roles—the fact that on Shakespeare's stage the women are really male. But the gender ambiguity relates as well to roles within the play—Lady Macbeth unsexes herself, and accuses her husband of being afraid to act like a man. What constitutes acting like a man in this play: what other than killing? Lady Macbeth unsexing herself renders herself, unexpectedly, not a man but a child, and thus incapable of murder: 'Had he not resembled/ My father as he slept, I had done't' (2.2.12–13). Indeed, the definitive relation between murder and manhood applies to heroes as well as villains. When Macduff is told of the murder of his wife and children and is urged to 'Dispute it like a man', he replies that he must first 'feel it as a man' (4.3.221–3). Whatever this says about his sensitivity and family feeling, it also says that murder is what makes you feel like a man.

The unsettling quality of the witches goes beyond gender. Their language is paradoxical; fair is foul and foul is fair; when the battle's lost and won. One way of looking at this is to say that it constitutes no paradox at all: any battle that is lost has also been won, but by somebody else. The person who describes a battle as lost and won is either on both sides or on neither; what is fair for one side is bound to be foul for the other. In a brilliantly subversive essay written as the millennium approached, Harry Berger, Jr., suggested that the witches are in fact right, and are telling the truth about the world of the play—that there really are no ethical standards in it, no right and wrong sides.[2] Duncan certainly starts out sounding like a good king: the rhetoric of his monarchy is full of claims about its sacredness, about the deference that is due to it, how it is part of a natural hierarchy descending from God, how the king is divinely anointed, and so forth. But in fact none of this is borne out by the play: Duncan's rule is utterly chaotic, and maintaining it depends on constant warfare— the battle that opens the play, after all, is not an invasion, but a rebellion. Duncan's rule has never commanded the deference it claims for itself—deference is not natural to it. In upsetting that sense of the deference Macbeth feels he owes to Duncan, maybe the witches are releasing into the play something the play both overtly denies and implicitly articulates: that there is no basis whatever for the values asserted on Duncan's behalf; that the primary characteristic of his rule, perhaps of any rule in the world of the play, is not order but rebellion.

Whether or not this is correct, it must be to the point that women are the ones who prompt this dangerous realization in Macbeth. The witches live outside the social order, but they embody its contradictions: beneath the woman's exterior is also a man; beneath the man's exterior is also a woman. Nature is full of competing claims, not ordered and hierarchical; to acknowledge that is to acknowledge the reality and force and validity of the individual will—to acknowledge that all of us have claims that conflict with royal claims about deference and hierarchy. This is the same recognition that Edmund brings into *King Lear* when he invokes Nature as his goddess. It is a Nature that is not the image of divine order, but one in which the strongest and craftiest survive—and when they survive, they then go on to devise claims about Nature that justify their success, claims about hierarchies, natural law and order, the divine right of kings. Edmund is a villain, but if he were ultimately successful he would be indistinguishable from the Duncans and Malcolms (and King Jameses) of Shakespeare's world.

Let us consider the implications of the addition to the play of the witches' songs and dances from Middleton. *The Witch* was written between 1610 and 1615; so by that time there was felt to be a need for more variety in the play, of a specifically theatrical kind, singing and dancing. I have suggested that witchcraft was good theatrical capital, but this does not really account for the revisions. Witchcraft was good theatre no matter what the witches did—spells, incantations, visions, appearances and disappearances, diabolical music were their stock in trade. It would not have been at all necessary to transform them into the vaudevillians that they become for Macbeth's entertainment. If the play required variety, Duncan's hosts could have entertained him at dinner as the King of Navarre entertains the Princess of France, with dances and a disguising; or Banquo's ghost, like Puck or Hamlet, could have interrupted a play within the play; or like Prospero, Duncan could have presented a royal masque to celebrate his son's investiture as Prince of Cumberland. Why bring the witches into it? But, to judge from the play's stage history, the vaudevillian witches constituted a stroke of theatrical genius.

Or did they? Consider the play's stage history. How successful, in fact, was *Macbeth* in its own time? Though it seems inconceivable that King James would not have been interested in the play, there is, as I have said, no record of a court performance—nor is there, in fact, a record of *any* pre-Restoration performance other than the one Simon Forman saw at the Globe in 1611, and reported in his diary. The *Shakespeare Allusion Book* records only seven other references to the play before 1649; of these, only three, all before 1611, are clearly allusions to performances. A fourth, from 1642, is quoting it as a classic text. The remaining examples merely refer to the historical figure of Macbeth, and need not derive from the play.[3] This, it must be emphasized, is a very small number of allusions: for comparison, there are fifty-eight to *Hamlet*, thirty-six to *Romeo and Juliet*, twenty-nine to the *Henry IV* plays, twenty-three to *Richard III*, nineteen to *Othello*.

This is all we know of the stage history of the play up to the Restoration. So perhaps reinventing the witches was not a stroke of theatrical genius after all; perhaps all it did was undertake, with uncertain success, to liven up an unpopular play. When Davenant revised *Macbeth* for the new stage, he inserted the whole of the singing and dancing scenes from Middleton—as I have indicated, this is at least arguably how the play had been performed on the public stage for two decades or more before the closing of the theatres in 1642, and it would thus have been this version of the play that Davenant saw throughout his youth. (Davenant was born in 1606, so he was going to theatre in the 1620s and 1630s). Indeed, since *The Witch* remained unpublished until 1778, it is likely that Davenant took his text not from Middleton at all, but directly from the King's Men's performance-text of *Macbeth*. Samuel Pepys provides a good testimony to the success of these and Davenant's other additions. Between 1664 and 1669 he went to the play nine times. The first time he found it only 'a pretty good play, but admirably acted'—the admirable Macbeth was Thomas Betterton at the outset of his career. What Pepys saw on this occasion was doubtless the folio text, with its Middleton additions. Thereafter he saw the play as Davenant refurbished it, and his response changed dramatically. It was, at various times, 'a most excellent play for variety'; 'a most excellent play in all respects, but especially in divertisement, though it be a deep tragedy; which is a strange perfection in a tragedy, it being most proper here and suitable'; and finally, 'one of the best plays for a stage, and a variety of dancing and music, that I ever saw.'[4]

The interesting point here is the relation between 'deep tragedy' and 'divertisement', which clearly for Pepys is a critical one. It is what he likes best about the play—indeed, it is what makes him revise his opinion of the play from 'pretty good' to 'most excellent'. And what Davenant added to the play—songs, dances, spectacle—is not simply something to appeal to Restoration taste. He expanded and elaborated elements that were already being added even before the folio text was published in 1623. So that is something to pause over: the really striking theatricality of the tragedy, its emphasis not just on visions and hallucinations, but on spectacle of all kinds, and even overtly—in scenes like the witches' dances—on entertainment, and its move toward the court masque. We see *Macbeth* as the most intensely inward of Shakespeare's plays, in which much of the action seems to take place within Macbeth's head, or as a projection of his fears and fantasies. But if we look again at the text we have, and fill in the blanks, we see that, as far back as our evidence goes, a great deal of the play's character was always determined by what Pepys called 'variety' and 'divertisement'. Perhaps for early audiences, then, these elements were not antithetical to psychological depth after all. In this respect *Macbeth* resembles *The Tempest* more than it does the other tragedies.

The play's 'divertisement' is a quality that is largely lost to us, partly because it is only hinted at in the folio text, which merely indicates that the songs are to be sung, but does not print them, and partly because it is so difficult to imagine doing the full-scale grotesque ballet they imply in a modern production. Pepys thought divertisement should have seemed radically indecorous too; but, to his surprise, he did not find it so. What is the relation between tragedy and the antic quality of the witches? Why does that antic quality keep increasing in size and importance in the stage history of the play from the seventeenth through the nineteenth century? Addison, for example, recalls his attention being distracted at a Betterton performance by a woman loudly asking 'When will the dear witches enter?';[5] Garrick, despite his claim to have returned to the text as originally written by Shakespeare, kept all Davenant's witch scenes; and in 1793, when Mrs Siddons was the Lady Macbeth, Hecate and her spirits descended and ascended on clouds, and the cauldron scene constituted a long interpolated pantomime.[6] Clearly Mrs Siddons did not think she was being upstaged. Can we imagine similar elements playing a similarly crucial role in the stage history of *King Lear* or *Hamlet*? In fact, we can: in *King Lear*, if it is the antic quality we are concerned with, there are Lear's mad scenes and the fool's zany speeches, which we find so hard to understand and pare down to a minimum, but which must have been popular in Shakespeare's time because new ones were added between the 1608 quarto and the 1623 folio. As for *Hamlet*, perhaps *Macbeth*'s witches externalize that anarchic quality that makes the prince so dangerous an adversary to the guilty king.

Suppose we try to imagine a *Hamlet* written from Claudius's point of view, in the way that *Macbeth* is written from Macbeth's. Look at it this way: the murder Claudius commits is the perfect crime; but the hero-villain quickly finds that his actions have unimagined implications, and that the world of politics is not all he has to contend with. Even as it stands, *Hamlet* is a very political play, and does not really need the ghost at all: Hamlet has his suspicions already; Claudius tries to buy him off by promising him the succession, but this is not good enough. It turns out that the problem is not really conscience or revenge, it is Hamlet's own ambitions—he says he wanted to succeed his father on the throne; Claudius, Hamlet says, 'Popped in between the election and my hopes' (5.2.640). The ghost is really, literally, a deus ex machina.

But in a *Hamlet* that did not centre on Hamlet, Claudius's guilty conscience, which is not much in evidence in the play, would have a great deal more work to do. So would the ghost—who should, after all, logically be haunting Claudius, not Hamlet. This play would be not about politics but about how the dead do not disappear, they return to embody our crimes, so that we have to keep repeating them—just like *Macbeth*. In this version of *Hamlet*, Hamlet is hardly necessary, any more than in *Macbeth*, Malcolm and Macduff are necessary—the drama of Macbeth is really a matter between Macbeth and his ambition, Macbeth, the witches, his wife, his hallucinations, and his own tortured soul; the drama of prophecies and riddles, how he understands them, what he decides to do about them, and how they, in themselves, constitute retribution.

What, then, about the riddles, those verbal incarnations of the imperfect speakers the witches? Macbeth is told that he will never be conquered till Birnam Wood comes to Dunsinane; and that no man of woman born will harm him. Are these paradoxical impossibilities realized? Not at all, really: the Birnam Wood prophecy does not come true, it just appears to Macbeth that it does—the wood is not moving, it merely looks as if it is. Or alternatively, we could say that 'Birnam Wood' is a quibble: Macbeth assumes it means the forest, but it could mean merely the branches the soldiers are using for camouflage, wood from the forest—it comes true merely as a stage device. As for 'no man of woman born', maybe the problem is that Macbeth is not a close enough reader: he takes the operative word to be 'woman'—'No man of *woman* born shall harm Macbeth'—but the key word turns out to be 'born'—'No man of woman *born* shall harm Macbeth'. If this is right, we must go on to consider the implications of the assumption that a Caesarean section does not constitute birth. This is really, historically, quite significant: a vaginal birth would have been handled by women, the midwife, maids, attendants, with no men present. But surgery was a male prerogative—the surgeon was always a man; midwives were not allowed to use surgical instruments—and the surgical birth thus means, in Renaissance terms, that Macduff was brought to life by men, not women: carried by a woman, but made viable only through masculine intervention. Such a birth, all but invariably, involved the mother's death.[7]

Macbeth himself sees it this way, when he defies Macduff and says,

... though Birnam Wood be come to Dunsinane,
And thou opposed being of no woman born ...

(5.10.30–1)

where logically it should be 'being not of woman born': the key concept is not 'no woman', but 'not born'. But Shakespeare seems to be conceiving of a masculine equivalent to the immaculate conception, a birth uncontaminated by women, as the Virgin's conception in her mother Saint Anne, and her own pregnancy, were uncontaminated by man.

So this riddle bears on the whole issue of the place of women in the play's world, how very disruptive they seem to be, even when, like Lady Macduff, they are loving and nurturing. Why is it so important, for example, at the end of the play, that Malcolm is a virgin? Malcolm insists to Macduff that he is utterly pure, 'as yet/ Unknown to woman' (4.3.126–7), uncontaminated by heterosexuality—this is offered as the first of his qualifications for displacing and succeeding Macbeth. Perhaps this bears too on the really big unanswered question about Macduff: why he left his family unprotected when he went to seek Malcolm in England—this is what makes Malcolm mistrust him so deeply. Why would you leave your wife and children unprotected, to face the tyrant's rage, unless you knew they were really in no danger?

But somehow the question goes unanswered, does not need to be answered, perhaps because Lady Macduff in some way is the problem, just as, more obviously, Lady Macbeth and the witches are. Those claims on Macduff that tie him to his wife and children, that would keep him at home, that purport to be higher than the claims of masculine solidarity, are in fact rejected quite decisively by the play. In Shakespeare's source in Holinshed's *Chronicles*, Macduff flees only *after* his wife and children have been murdered, and therefore for the best of reasons. Macduff's desertion of his family is Shakespeare's addition to the story. Maybe, the play keeps saying, if it weren't for all those women …? It really is an astonishingly male-oriented and misogynistic play, especially at the end, when there are simply no women left, not even the witches, and the restored commonwealth is a world of heroic soldiers. Is the answer to Malcolm's question about why Macduff left his family, 'Because it's *you* I really love'?

So, to return to the increasingly elaborate witches' scenes, the first thing they do for this claustrophobic play is to open up a space for women; and it is a subversive and paradoxical space. This is a play in which paradoxes abound, and for Shakespeare's audience, Lady Macbeth would have embodied those paradoxes as powerfully as the witches do: in her proclaimed ability to 'unsex' herself, in her willingness to dash her own infant's brains out, but most of all, in the kind of control she exercises over her husband. The marriage at the centre of the play is one of the most frightening things about it, but it is worth observing that, as Shakespearean marriages go, this is a good one: intense, intimate, loving. The notion that your wife is your friend and your comfort is not a Shakespearean one. The relaxed, easygoing, happy time men and women have together in Shakespeare all takes place before marriage, as part of the wooing process—this is the subject of comedy. What happens after marriage is the subject of tragedy—Goneril and Regan are only extreme versions of perfectly normative Shakespearean wives. The only Shakespearean marriage of any duration that is represented as specifically sexually happy is the marriage of Claudius and Gertrude, a murderer and an adulteress; and it is probably to the point that even they stop sleeping together after only four months—not, to be sure, by choice.

8

The Folio

Throughout the sixteenth century the folio, the largest standard book size, was the format for serious works of philosophy, history and science; and also for the classics, the body of learning that the Renaissance saw itself as bringing back to life. Folios were expensive to produce and therefore to buy; the market for them was limited to those with the means to acquire them, the space to store them, and the time to appreciate them—though the survival rate of these huge volumes suggests that they did not get much use. Ben Jonson, collecting his work and issuing it as a folio in 1616 was making a radical statement both for himself and for literature in English. The English poetic classics that had previously appeared in folio were the works of Chaucer, Gower, and Lydgate, books written in the fourteenth and fifteenth centuries, before the religious revolution effected by Henry VIII. After that, Chaucer, Gower, and the proto-Protestant Langland were the only literature in English from the Catholic past that was permitted to be sold and read (Lydgate's *Fall of Princes* was considered dangerously topical, and was banned until the reign of Elizabeth I). Moreover, before 1616 only one living English author had published his literary works in folio, Samuel Daniel, in 1601.

But Jonson's model was not the Daniel folio; it was the great sixteenth-century editions of the Greek and Roman dramatists. The Ben Jonson first folio, issued in 1616 and edited by Jonson himself, was titled *The Workes of Benjamin Jonson*. The first section consisted of plays. This caused surprise and some disapproval. Jonson was criticized for including his plays in a volume of works:

To Mr. Ben Johnson, demanding the reason why he call'd his playes works.
Pray tell me *Ben*, where doth the mystery lurke,
What others call a play, you call a worke.¹

Plays for the popular stage were not 'works'. But Jonson insisted that his plays were Works, and the folio declared him a classic. Indeed, soon enough the format itself was a guarantee of quality. In 1610 Sir Thomas Bodley warned his first librarian Thomas James not to acquire for Oxford's Bodleian Library any 'riffe-raffes' and 'baggage books', in which he included almanacs, pamphlets and 'Englishe plaies'. The library, however, not only acquired the Shakespeare first folio in 1623, but provided a special binding for its copy.² This probably does not indicate any change of heart about plays, but it certainly acknowledges the dignity of the format—a folio was not a 'riffe-raffe'. In 1664, the library replaced the volume with the second issue of the third folio, which includes seven additional plays that had been credited to Shakespeare in his lifetime: the most desirable edition was not the first edition, but the newest and most comprehensive one, and the library now wanted to be up to date with its Shakespeare plays. (By 1910, when first folios had become seriously valuable, the library bought back its original copy for £3,000, the highest price it had ever paid for a book.)³

The Jonson folio was a precedent for the Shakespeare folio, but not a model for it, though it certainly provided a model for treating English plays as serious literature. Jonson's publisher was lavish with paper: the text, except for a brief section near the end, is in single columns. It is a self-consciously handsome book, with a great deal of white space. The Shakespeare volume looks crowded in comparison; it has fewer pages, though it comprises more text. It is a great deal less lavish with layout and margins, and though because of an extended interruption it took even longer to print, it was notably successful. The interruption occurred during the printing of *Richard II*—that is, in the middle of the Histories—and lasted for almost a year, during which the printers produced two other volumes, both of which were expected to sell quickly, and did so. The Shakespeare folio was a longer-term investment, and they were in no hurry to finish.

For the publisher and printers, the Shakespeare folio certainly represented a better investment than the Jonson folio: a second edition was warranted after only nine years, whereas there was no call for a new Jonson folio for twenty-four years, and none after that until 1692. Edward Blount, the publisher of the Shakespeare folio, transferred his rights to Robert Allott in 1630, probably simply because he and the printers decided to retire. Allott's second folio appeared in 1632. It is not clear how successful the second folio was: there was no third folio until 1663, though there is some evidence that Allott's volume was reissued in 1641.[4] The Shakespeare folio was, probably inevitably, much less carefully produced than the Jonson folio, since the author was not involved. The two books are also significantly unlike in that the Shakespeare folio is very clearly not Works, and does not claim to be: it is *Mr. William Shakespeares Comedies, Histories, & Tragedies*. Shakespeare in his own time was best known to the reading public as the poet of *Venus and Adonis* and *Lucrece*, but the canonical collection of his writings in the seventeenth century, preserved in the first four folios, included only plays.

The Shakespeare folio was designed to be a very expensive book, but with its double-column text it looks significantly less lavish than the Jonson folio. It was also much less carefully proofread, including about 500 press corrections, one-fifth of the Jonson folio's—the latter, of course, included not only corrections, but also Jonson's revisions. Nevertheless, the Shakespeare volume clearly had much less editorial care. The printing of the book was also afflicted with problems. *Troilus and Cressida* had originally been placed after *Romeo and Juliet*—despite the quarto's characterization of the play as 'full of the palme comicall' and like 'the best commedy in Terence or Plautus', for the folio editors it was a tragedy: certainly it does not end happily. But during the printing of the section of tragedies a problem was encountered with the rights to the play, and it was removed. Assuming that the rights would eventually be obtained, the printers calculated the number of pages the play would require, and continued printing with *Julius Caesar*. By the time the rest of the volume was complete, however, the business of *Troilus* remained unresolved, and its space was filled with a much shorter play, *Timon of Athens* (now considered a collaboration with Thomas Middleton), which had almost certainly never been performed. The result was a gap of eleven pages in the numbering between the end of *Timon* and the beginning of *Julius Caesar*.

But after the printing of the preliminaries, which were normally done last, the rights to *Troilus* were finally negotiated, and it was re-inserted at the beginning of the tragedy section, where the page numbering started over at 1—this was as close as possible to its original position, but it meant that *Coriolanus*, which originally began the tragedies, was now preceded by *Troilus and Cressida*, the first three pages of which had already been printed, with the first page unnumbered, but the second and third numbered 79 and 80 (the last page of *Romeo and Juliet* is 77, though to accommodate the new *Troilus* it had to be reprinted and was erroneously numbered 79). Even this was problematic: the original text had been simply a reprint of the 1609 quarto; the restored text was a different one, with many variants from the quarto, and most significantly, with a page-long prologue, which is not in the quarto and was not in the play as it was first being printed in the folio. But since the play originally began on a verso with a blank recto, the new prologue was printed there, in large type with very large margins, to take up most of the page. It was simply headed, however, 'The Prologue', with no indication of what it is the prologue to. The three original pages follow, with the remainder unnumbered after 79 and 80; and *Coriolanus* then begins on a page numbered 1. *Troilus and Cressida* is not listed in the volume's table of contents, which would have been printed before the play was finally included.

There are also problematic elements in the design of the huge volume. Jonson's chronological organization had made sense as the author's presentation of his own career. Such an arrangement would probably not have been possible for Shakespeare's editors, requiring more information about the history of the plays' composition than they had; but except in the case of the histories, the generic arrangement is really a grab-bag, with the order of the comedies and tragedies reflecting only the order in which the plays were made ready for the press. And though the histories are organized according to the dates of the reigns involved, even that has its arbitrary element: the sequence covers the century from the reign of Richard II to that of Richard III, but with the much earlier *King John* tacked onto the beginning and the later *Henry VIII* at the end; and with the plays about still earlier British history, *King Lear* and *Cymbeline*, moved into the section of tragedies.

Even the classicizing of the texts by adding acts and scenes was haphazard. The quartos have none. The folio supplies most of the histories with acts, but only occasionally with scenes; and in the second and third parts of *Henry VI* with no act and scene divisions whatever after the opening announcement *Actus Primus. Scæna Prima*. In the tragedies *Hamlet*, as we have seen, has acts and scenes until 2.2, and not thereafter. The Roman plays *Titus Andronicus*, *Julius Caesar* and *Coriolanus* have acts and no scenes; but *Anthony and Cleopatra* has only the initial *Actus Primus. Scæna Prima*. So do *Romeo and Juliet* and *Timon of Athens*, but *King Lear*, *Othello* and *Cymbeline* have the full complement. Of the comedies, the first three plays *The Tempest*, *The Merry Wives of Windsor* and *Measure for Measure* have both acts and scenes; and thereafter most have acts but no scenes, with the exception of *As You Like It*, *Twelfth Night* and *The Winter's Tale*, which have both. (Act divisions may be original in plays for the private theatres—thus *The Tempest* at the end of Act 4 has Prospero onstage, and at the beginning of Act 5 has him entering. This might mean that a scene is missing, but it is more likely that it indicates a pause in the action, to be filled, for example, with music.)

Certain idiosyncratic elements allow us to identify the scribe who prepared *The Tempest* and four other comedies for the folio as Ralph Crane, a scrivener whom the King's Men occasionally employed as a copyist. Several plays from the period (though none by Shakespeare), and a variety of other manuscripts, survive in his hand. The first play in the folio is *The Tempest*, probably simply because it was prepared first, apparently by Crane. It exemplifies the transformation of plays into reading texts: there are massed entries at the beginning of every scene, with no indication of when in the scene characters enter—this is the way classical drama had been presented from the earliest manuscript sources, and was the convention used by Jonson in his folio. When the plays in the Shakespeare folio are provided with scenes, they have been classicized in this way. But *The Tempest* goes further: at significant points stage directions are narrative rather than directive, such as this in 3.3

> *Solemne and strange Musicke: and Prosper on the top (invisible:) Enter severall strange shapes, bringing in a Banket, and dance about it with gentle actions of salutations, and inviting the King, etc. to eate, they depart.*

And this in Act 5:

> *Heere enters* Ariel *before: Then* Alonso *with a franticke gesture, attended by* Gonzalo. Sebastian *and* Antonio *in like manner attended by* Adrian *and* Francisco: *They all enter the circle which* Prospero *had made, and there stand charm'd; which* Prospero *observing, speakes.*

In the latter example, a script would require a stage direction for Prospero to draw the circle some lines before this; here there is none. But if this was intended as a model for presenting Shakespeare's drama as a narrative for readers, the model was abandoned after *The Tempest* even in those plays that Crane transcribed.

Shakespeare's portrait in the 1623 folio was by Martin Droeshout, a young and inexperienced artist. At Shakespeare's death, in 1616, he was fifteen years old; he was twenty-two when the folio was published, and this image is, so far as we know, his first commissioned work. If the engraving derives from a portrait made from life, the portrait must have been done by someone else and Droeshout must have adapted it many years later (the Shakespeare of the portrait looks to be in his thirties; so this is Shakespeare around 1600). In fact, Droeshout's presence on the title page of this elaborately produced, expensive book is a puzzle. The portraits included in similar volumes in the period are for the most part provided by a small group of very accomplished artists: Simon van de Passe, Cornelis Boel, William Hole, Robert Vaughan, William Marshall.[5] Moreover, the very fact that the portrait is on the title page is puzzling. Normally the author's portrait, especially if it is engraved, will be facing the title page, as a frontispiece—especially if it is engraved, because it is difficult to combine typesetting and engraving on the same page. If the portrait had been a woodcut, there would have been no problem: woodcuts can be printed on the same press with, and at the same time as, type. Engravings, however, require a different printing technique, and the Shakespeare title page therefore would have had to go through two separate processes. The usual way of dealing with this, if one wanted an engraving on the title page, was to engrave the whole page, as was done for the Jonson folio, Drayton's *Poly-Olbion* (1613), King James's *Workes* (1616), Chapman's Homer (1611/1616), and innumerable other large, important, expensive books. The publishers of Shakespeare were making trouble for themselves.

Opposite the title page, where the frontispiece would normally go, is a poem in large type—this, technically, is the frontispiece.[6] The poem is addressed To the Reader, and urges us to ignore the portrait:

> This Figure, that thou here seest put,
> It was for gentle Shakespeare cut;
> Wherein the Graver had a strife
> with Nature, to out-doo the life:
> O, could he but have drawne his wit
> As well in brasse, as he hath hit
> His face, the Print would then surpasse
> All, that was ever writ in brasse.
> But, since he cannot, Reader, looke
> Not on his Picture, but his Booke.

'Looke/ Not on his Picture, but his Booke': the poem construes the portrait and the book as alternatives, or even adversaries. The poem is signed only with the initials B. I., and has always been credited to Ben Jonson. This is doubtless correct, but it is worth remarking that Jonson's other dedicatory poem in the volume is signed in his characteristic way, Ben: Ionson, and Jonson did not subsequently include the poem anywhere among his works. In effect, he disowned the poem in the course of dismissing Shakespeare's portrait.

Establishing a canon

It has been suggested that for the publisher Edward Blount, the Shakespeare folio was a bad investment, and even that it bankrupted him because by 1630 he had sold his rights in the book to Robert Allott and was out of business, but it is more likely that Blount, who was nearing 70, simply decided to retire—his printer William Jaggard had died in 1623, and Jaggard's son Isaac, who succeeded him, had died in 1627. Allott clearly considered the Shakespeare folio a valuable property, since he had it reprinted very quickly; it was published in 1632. The second folio, moreover, was firmly modelled on the first, basically a page-for-page reprint, retaining even the dangling Prologue to *Troilus and Cressida*. But not entirely: in addition to a large number of minor editorial adjustments, it corrects mistakes in Holofernes's Latin in *Love's Labour's Lost*. There is doubtless some pedantry on display in this, but one may wonder what the editor thought was being corrected. Are the mistakes Shakespeare's, or those of the scribe who prepared the play for the press, or of the first compositor incorrectly transcribing a correct manuscript? Or are the mistakes perfectly correct, and is the point that Holofernes's Latin is at fault?

Whether the second folio was a good investment for Allott is unclear. It was perhaps reissued in 1641,[7] but no new edition was called for until 1663, more than twenty years later; and even then, a simple reissue of the book turned out to sell poorly. A year later the volume was republished with seven additional plays that had been credited to Shakespeare in his lifetime—more Shakespeare was more desirable Shakespeare (and the Bodleian Library duly replaced its first folio). This in fact is the rarest of the folios, since a good deal of the stock was destroyed in the London fire of 1666. But in a striking piece of cultural pathology, it was the first folio that ultimately became the seriously valuable one, and the basis of the Shakespeare canon.

The first folio is not at all a rare book. It was published in 1623 in an edition of about 750 copies, of which 233 copies survive; 53 of these are considered complete, including all blanks and preliminaries.[8] That is a large survival rate for a book of the period, and suggests that the book was more treasured than read. For comparison, there are many fewer surviving copies of the Gutenberg bible, an even more iconic book that constitutes the beginning of printing in the western world. It was published in 1455; there now exist 48 copies, 20 of them complete. And Gutenberg bibles, unlike Shakespeare folios, are really hard to come by—the last complete copy came up for sale in 1978. It is often claimed that only one copy of the Shakespeare first folio remains in private hands, the implication being that they are impossible to buy; but in fact, institutions sell their copies fairly regularly, and one comes up at auction on average every five years. Recent auction prices for the book have ranged from about $6 million to almost $10 million—the last one sold at Christie's in 2020 for $9,978,000. There are of course no comparable recent sale figures for the Gutenberg bible, but the complete one that sold in 1978 cost $2.2 million, and in 1984 an incomplete copy, just the Old Testament, sold for $5.4 million—allowing for inflation, that is more than the Shakespeare folio figures, but of the same order of magnitude. A more informative comparison, however, is with the Nuremberg Chronicle, published in 1493, one of the great monuments of early printing, where the survival figures are about the same as those for the Shakespeare folio. That not-very-rare book comes up for sale frequently. At the annual California book fair there are always two or three copies to be had, usually priced between $90,000 and $150,000.[9]

Obviously the Shakespeare folio is a more desirable book—how much more desirable is indicated by another unusual thing about it: that serious collectors have often wanted to own multiple copies. The Folger Library in Washington has the most by far, at 82; Meisei University in Tokyo has twelve; the New York Public Library six, the British Library five, the Huntington Library four. (Interestingly, the first purchaser of whom we have a record, Sir Edward Dering, in December 1623, a week or so after publication, bought two copies.) It is true that not all copies of the folio are identical—that is true of most books published before the eighteenth century—but they are certainly all the same book, and if you were spending many millions to establish your cultural sophistication, surely one copy would be enough. (Henry Clay Folger's desire for multiple copies was reasonable, in that he was interested specifically in the text of Shakespeare, and believed, correctly, that only by comparing many copies could a proper text be finally established.) In contrast, the Nuremberg Chronicle is a much more interesting piece of printing, but libraries do not pride themselves on how many copies they own.

The first folio's price remained fairly stable until the middle of the eighteenth century—there was a new edition of Shakespeare every ten years or so in that period, but editors based their texts on the fourth folio. The return to the first folio as the best text came only after 1760, when Samuel Johnson, preparing his great edition, called attention to the many errors in the fourth folio. After that, the first folio was the 'right' folio, and its value began to increase. In 1756 a copy sold for a little over £3; by 1790 the going price was £35. By the beginning of the twentieth century a first folio cost between $5,000 and $10,000—not, by this time, because scholars needed it to work from, but because millionaires, especially Americans, with cultural aspirations, wanted it in their collections. At the same time, Shakespeare became a subject of study at universities—the first Shakespeare courses were taught in American and British universities beginning in the 1870s.[10] Shakespeare had become the touchstone of English literacy.

Michael Dobson, director of the Shakespeare Institute in Stratford-Upon-Avon, sums it up this way: 'during the eighteenth century the folio became the holy book of a new secular religion, bardolatry, . . . and by the late nineteenth century, the first folio was a natural destination for the excess profits of Anglophone millionaires, keen to own symbolic capital in the culture in which they have flourished.'[11] The astonishing rise in the book's value is part of the history of both American conspicuous consumption and American public benevolence: Dobson writes:

> [T]he surviving Folios have migrated over time from private collections in Britain to privately endowed public ones in North America. In 1902, of 158 known copies, 100 were in the UK, 39 in the USA; today, of 228, there are 44 in Britain and 145 in the

States. . . . Between 1893 and 1928 Henry Clay Folger, president of Standard Oil, bought no fewer than 79.[12]

The Folger Library is thus the great monument to that migration, but it was designed to be much more: Dobson observes that Folger opened his library 'in 1932 on a site in the middle of Washington DC carefully selected to be on the line that joins the Lincoln Memorial, the Washington Monument, the Capitol and the Supreme Court—as if to write bardolatry into the American Constitution itself'.[13]

Inventing romance

The new plays that were added to the second issue of the third folio included six that eventually again disappeared from the canon; but the seventh, *Pericles*, ultimately became a staple of the Shakespeare repertory, the first of the genre of romances. This new Shakespearean category was created by Edward Dowden in 1877:

> There is a romantic element about these plays. In all there is the same romantic incident of lost children recovered by those to whom they are dear—the daughters of Pericles and Leontes, the sons of Cymbeline and Alonso. In all there is a beautiful romantic background of sea or mountain. The dramas have a grave beauty, a sweet serenity, which seem to render the name 'comedies' inappropriate; we may smile tenderly, but we never laugh loudly, as we read them. Let us, then, name this group consisting of four plays, Romances.[14]

Strictly speaking, however, *Pericles* is the only play that really fits the category, a play about a knight who travels the world having adventures, always on the edge of tragedy, but never tragic thanks to a series of happy, utterly improbable coincidences, and who is ultimately rescued by magic and miracle. *Pericles* had been one of Shakespeare's most popular plays in his own time, for readers as well as theatregoers: it went through six quarto editions by 1635, and earned a sneer from Jonson as a 'mouldy tale'.[15] Its absence from the folio may have been a matter of rights, but the folio compilers may have known that it was a collaborative play (as most modern scholars believe), and omitted it as they omitted *The Two Noble Kinsmen*, Shakespeare's acknowledged collaboration with John Fletcher. On the other hand, several plays that we believe were collaborative—the first two parts of *Henry VI*, *Measure for Measure*, *Timon of Athens*, *Henry VIII*, and *Macbeth* (which acknowledges its non-Shakespearean material in its text)—are in the folio, and the editors may simply not have had access to a satisfactory text of *Pericles*.

It is worth pausing over the belated inclusion of *Pericles* in the canon, since the play figures so significantly in the construction of the modern Shakespeare. The seven plays added to the folio in 1664 were, in addition to *Pericles*, *The Yorkshire Tragedy*, *The Puritan Widow*, *Locrine*, *Thomas Lord Cromwell*, *The London Prodigal* and *Sir John Oldcastle*. In this, the editors were both selective and haphazard: there were several more plays credited to Shakespeare in his lifetime that they missed, and in at least one case they apparently did not read beyond the title page: *Sir John Oldcastle* declares in a prefatory note that it is not by Shakespeare, and is in fact correcting the version of Oldcastle presented in Shakespeare's character, Falstaff. Nevertheless, the 1619 quarto of the play published by Thomas Pavier and William Jaggard has Shakespeare's name on the title page—the original 1600 quarto does not—and that was enough to make it Shakespeare in 1664.[16]

Over the next century, the seven plays moved in and out of the Shakespeare canon. Nicholas Rowe in 1709 included them in his edition. Pope banished them in 1725, but his publisher included them in the second edition of Pope's Shakespeare three years later—more Shakespeare was more marketable Shakespeare, and purchasers of a complete Shakespeare might be willing to replace it with a more complete Shakespeare. Edmond Malone in 1780 settled the matter for later editors by rejecting all but *Pericles*: there was something in Malone's idea of Shakespeare that did not suit with six of the seven plays (and he would have read beyond the title page of *Sir John Oldcastle*). But *Pericles* was another matter: there was by 1780 something in *Pericles* that the idea of Shakespeare could not do without. What that something was, however, changed a number of times over the next two centuries.

We might assume that what Malone considered necessarily Shakespearean in it was its claims to transcendence, its affinities with *Anthony and Cleopatra* and *The Winter's Tale*—in short, its 'lateness'— but those only became part of the play's character a century later: for Malone it was—*self-evidently* (this is worth emphasizing)—an early play, one of Shakespeare's earliest: he dated it 1592.[17] For Malone, *Pericles* was Shakespeare before he became Shakespeare (rather like the current critical status of *Edward III*).

It remained an early play until 1839, when John Payne Collier called attention to a reference to a performance of *Pericles* in 1608 that described the play as new. He also cited George Wilkins's novel *The Painful Adventures of Pericles Prince of Tyre*, published in 1608, which declares itself based on the play, and has significant verbal similarities to it. Subsequently, however, Collier had his own doubts, deciding that *Pericles* was in fact an early play that Shakespeare reworked. This was the line that most critics thereafter took, until late in the century, when Edward Dowden declared it the first of the late plays, and invented the category of romances for them.

In devising the drama of Shakespeare's career, *Pericles* gave Malone a beginning and Dowden an ending. We have completely bought into Dowden's idea of romance as an authentically Shakespearean genre— the less anachronistic category of tragicomedy has had little attraction for us, though many of Shakespeare's comedies and all the works we think of as 'problem plays' would fit comfortably into it. It is not a classical genre, though it is certainly a Renaissance one, and Italian theorists had justified it through an energetic critical debate. Jonson the classicist not only accommodated tragicomedy to his dramatic art, but elevated it to the top of the triumphal arch in his folio frontispiece.

Modern conceptions of genre are different from those of the Renaissance. Our categories are exclusive and definitive; theirs tended to be inclusive and analytic. For the Renaissance critic, to find a new category for a play was not to abandon the old ones. Julius Caesar Scaliger calls the *Oresteia* both a tragedy and a comedy, just as the quarto of *Troilus and Cressida* compares the play to those of Plautus and Terence, while for the folio editors it was a tragedy. In their historical context, these claims do not contradict each other. We have adopted the category of romance because we believe that certain kinds of seriousness are inappropriate to comedy, and because it gives us a way of accounting for the late plays' commitment to non-realistic modes. We have thereby shed light on the relation of four late plays to each other, but we have also thereby obscured their relation to the rest of Shakespearean drama.[18]

In fact, the 'sweet serenity' that for Dowden characterized his four romances omitted a great deal. The villains at the end of *The Tempest* are firmly unrepentant; *Cymbeline* concludes with some (not all) of the evil characters safely dead, but also with a king who acknowledges the radical fallibility of his judgment; there are losses at the end of *The Winter's Tale* that the unveiling of Hermione and the finding of Perdita cannot restore—the dead son and heir Mamillius, the lost husband and faithful servant Antigonus. Shakespearean comedy is often tragicomedy: *The Merchant of Venice*, *Much Ado About Nothing*, *Measure for Measure*. Even the sunny comedy of *As You Like It* opens with banishment and family conflicts, and in John Fletcher's *The Tamer Tamed*, a sequel to *The Taming of the Shrew*, Kate is dead within two years of her dubiously happy marriage. Much of *Anthony and*

Cleopatra is comic. Shakespeare turned the story of *King Lear* into a tragedy, violating both history and the play's own expectations; and it has often been observed that the tragedy of *Othello* has the structure of a comedy. A morbidly jealous husband, egged on by a clever, malicious underling, accuses his wife of infidelity, and when it is shown that he is mistaken repents. The conclusion could be simply 'The underling is punished and Othello promises not to be jealous any more'.

Conclusion

In an essay called 'A New Theater Historicism' Andrew Gurr observes that 'almost no play-texts survive from the Shakespearean time in a form that represents with much precision what was actually staged'.

> Out of the total of 167 extant plays performed by the Chamberlain's/King's Men in the 48 years that they played, the 'allowed book' or licensed playbook, the version from which performances were drawn and from which performances deviated only in special cases, survives in only two nearly complete play-manuscripts. Neither of them is by Shakespeare. That is less than two per cent of the total existing repertory of the leading company of the time. So the current shift of editorial target from the author's copy untouched by theater hacks to the script as it was first staged, which is the announced aim of the collected Oxford edition of 1986 and of almost all subsequent editions and series of editions, must be acknowledged to be unattainable.[1]

Let us return to Humphrey Moseley's introductory epistle to the 1647 Beaumont and Fletcher folio (see Chapter 1):

> When these *Comedies* and *Tragedies* were presented on the Stage, the *Actours* omitted some *Scenes* and Passages (with the *Authour's* consent) as occasion led them ... But now you have both All that was *Acted*, and all that was not; even the perfect full Originalls without the least mutilation; So that were the *Authours* living ... they themselves would challenge neither more nor lesse then what is here published ....[2]

A printed text, in Moseley's account, is a conflation of authors' and players' versions. The implication is that cuts were determined by the occasion: actors varied their performances according to their sense of the audience; they might change from season to season, from playhouse to playhouse, even, if occasion required, from performance to performance. The play before the king was not the same as the play at the Globe, and neither of them was the text that came from the authors. But most editors and critics go to extraordinary lengths to avoid dealing with the notion that our printed texts are not what Shakespeare's actors spoke, and that the script was always in flux.

But if the text was not the play, what was the relationship between the two? What kind of authority did Shakespeare's manuscript have, and what kind of responsibility did playhouse practice feel toward it? Shakespeare seems, in *Hamlet*, to be especially concerned about the dangers of improvisation:

> Let those that play your clowns speak no more than is set down for them. For there be of them that will themselves laugh, to set on some quantity of barren spectators to laugh too, though in the meantime some necessary question of the play be then to be considered.
>
> (3.2.42ff.)

But in Hamlet's first scene with the ghost, Hamlet's own behaviour, the jokes about the voice in the 'cellerage' and all the rushing about the stage to avoid the 'old mole' beneath will look to an audience without access to the script like a particularly disruptive kind of comic improvisation. This is Shakespeare making the anti-textual textual, but it also puts Shakespeare the actor in league with the audience against Shakespeare the playwright, and it strikingly reveals a divided loyalty.

Clearly there has always been a tension between text and performance, and as editors and critics we share, in profound and unexamined ways, that original divided loyalty. There is, of course, very little evidence that will reveal to us the nature of a performing text in Shakespeare's theatre; but there is a little. There are the 'bad' quartos, whose evidence is sometimes excellent—remember *Hamlet* Q1's stage directions about the ghost appearing in his nightgown and Ophelia with her hair down playing the lute. If we were less exclusively concerned with establishing texts and more concerned with the nature of plays, *Hamlet* Q1 would be a good quarto. More direct evidence survives in three pre-Restoration prompt-books, of *Macbeth*, *Measure for Measure* and the two parts of *Henry IV*.[3] The first two are marked up texts in a folio, the third is a scribal transcription based on the quartos. The *Henry IV* dates from the early 1620s, and was therefore composed before the folio was in print. It was prepared for a private production at the country estate of Sir Edward Dering, the first purchaser of record of the Shakespeare folio (he bought two copies). It underwent far more radical revision than the other two, amalgamating the two plays and reducing their approximately 6,000 lines to roughly 3,500, but also including additional original material. It reveals a great deal about both the sophistication of amateur theatre and the way a popular Shakespeare text was regarded by an enthusiastic admirer in the early seventeenth century; but it also represents a special case, and is therefore less useful for my purposes than the other two.

The prompt-books are preserved in a Shakespeare first folio now in the library of the University of Padua. Two plays, *Macbeth* and *Measure for Measure*, have been marked up for performance.[4] The book came to Padua in the mid-seventeenth century, the gift of the British consul in the Veneto the merchant John Hobson, along with treatises on mathematics, navigation, and commerce, and Sir John Harington's translation of *Orlando Furioso*—a gentleman's library. (The university acquired the books around 1840.) The editing of the two marked up plays has been dated to before 1640; they were prepared, according to G. Blakemore Evans, by a professional hand for a professional company. About their actual use we can say nothing, but they allow us to see what a performing text of Shakespeare looked like within a couple of decades of the playwright's death.

The editing throughout is designed to speed up action and reduce dialogue, not to clarify or simplify.[5] A great deal of what is most characteristically Shakespearean—poetic imagery, metaphorical complexity—is cut, including what have become some of the most famous passages in the two plays. In *Macbeth*, there are small and apparently arbitrary cuts in the first act. Moments in the text that have troubled later editors, such as the notorious muddle of the Captain's account of the battle, are left intact; indeed, the only cut before 1.7 is Macbeth's 'Present fears/ Are less than horrible imaginings' after he and Banquo meet the witches. But here is Macbeth's first soliloquy as it appears in the prompt-book:

> If it were done when 'tis done, then 'twere well
> It were done quickly: If th'Assassination
> Could trammell up the Consequence, and catch
> With his surcease, Successe: that but this blow
> Might be the be all, and the end all.
> Hee's heere in double trust;
> First, as I am his Kinsman, and his Subject,
> Strong both against the Deed: Then, as his Host,
> Who should against his Murtherer shut the doore,
> Not beare the knife my selfe. Besides, this *Duncane*
> Hath borne his Faculties so meeke: hath bin
> So cleere in his great Office, that his Vertues
> Will pleade like Angels, Trumpet-tongu'd against
> The deepe damnation of his taking off:
> And Pitty, like a naked New-borne-babe,
> Striding the blast, or Heavens Cherubin, hors'd
> Upon the sightlesse Curriors of the Ayre,
> Shall blow the horrid deed in every eye,
> That teares shall drowne the wind.
>
> *Enter Lady.*

What is cut from this is the bank and shoal of time, the bloody instructions, the poisoned chalice, the spur to prick the sides of my intent, the vaulting ambition that o'erleaps itself. And in the ensuing exchange between Macbeth and his wife, a large chunk of Lady Macbeth's persuasive rhetoric is deleted.

Wholesale cutting begins in Act 2. All of the Porter's speech goes (as it often has done since); with it go most of the exchange between Macbeth and the murderers, the whole of 3.6 between Lenox and the Lord, most of Malcolm's interview with Macduff, in which Malcolm tests Macduff by claiming to practice monstrous vices. In all, 292 of the play's 2,084 lines are cut, almost fifteen per cent. I want to pause over two other deletions.

As the play draws to its climax, Macbeth's response to the servant's news that the English forces are in sight has been radically simplified. He calls for Seyton, and says only this:

> *Seyton*, I am sick at hart
> When I behold: *Seyton*, I say—

thereby omitting what has become one of the most famous passages in the play

> I have liv'd long enough, my way of life
> Is falne into the Seare, the yellow Leafe,
> And that which should accompany Old-Age,
> As Honor, Love, Obedience, Troopes of Friends,
> I must not looke to have: but in their steed,
> Curses, not lowd but deepe, Mouth-honor, breath
> Which the poore heart would faine deny, and dare not.
>
> (5.3.19–28)

And Macbeth's reply to Seyton's report of the death of Lady Macbeth reads this way in the Padua text:

> She should have dy'de heereafter:
> There would have beene a time for such a word:
> To morrow, and to morrow, and to morrow,
> Creepes in this petty pace from day to day,

> To the last Syllable of Recorded time:
> And all our yesterdayes, have lighted Fooles
> The way to dusty death. Out, out, breefe Candle,
> Life's but a walking Shadow.
> It is a Tale
> Told by an Ideot, full of sound and fury
> Signifying nothing.

What is for us a characteristically Shakespearean bit of self-referentiality, the poor player who struts and frets his hour upon the stage and then is heard no more, is deleted.

The cutting of the Padua folio's *Measure for Measure* is far more systematic. A certain quality of continuous explanation in the play (a quality that most modem readers would call essential) disappears: gone are the Duke's opening speech ('Of government the properties to unfold ...'), the first fifteen lines of his charge to Angelo ('There is a kind of character in thy life/ That to th'observer doth thy history/ Fully unfold', etc.), and, more strikingly, Claudio's exculpatory account of why he and Juliet never formalized their marriage, 'This came we not to, Onely for propagation of a Dowre....' Indeed, even Claudio's revelation of Juliet's pregnancy, the source of all Claudio's trouble, was originally cut, but this was subsequently restored with a marginal 'stet'. Much of the Duke's explanation to the Friar of why he left his throne has gone, unquestionably to the benefit of his logic, if not to the complexity of his character. In Isabella's first interview with Angelo, the arguments on both sides are effectively eviscerated; indeed, the omission from this production of what were to become the most famous passages in the play is notable. Gone are Isabella's 'There is a vice that most I doe abhorre' speech, her passage about 'No ceremony that to great ones longs', her observation that 'all the soules that were, were forfeit once', and Angelo's reply that 'It is the Law, not I, condemne your brother'. Gone too is Isabella's 'Could great men thunder/ As *Jove* himselfe do's ...', including the famous passage

> man, proud man,
> Drest in a little briefe authoritie,
> Most ignorant of what he's most assur'd,
> (His glassie Essence) like an angry Ape
> Plaies such phantastique tricks before high heaven
> As makes the Angels weepe: who with our spleenes
> Would all themselves laugh mortall.
>
> (2.2.117–23)

After this it is no surprise to find Angelo's final soliloquy reading this way:

> What's this? what's this? is this her fault, or mine?
> The Tempter or the Tempted, who sins most? ha?
> Not she: nor doth she tempt: but it is I.
> What dost thou, or what art thou, Angelo? . . .
>
> (162ff.)

What has been omitted is, for the modern reader, the most distinctive moment in the speech:

> [it is I]
> That, lying by the Violet in the Sunne,
> Doe as the Carrion do's, not as the flowre,
> Corrupt with virtuous season. Can it be
> That Modesty may more betray our sense
> Then womans lightnesse? having waste ground enough,
> Shall we desire to raze the Sanctuary
> And pitch our evils there? Oh, fie, fie, fie:

The whole play is treated in this way. The only major scene that is left even relatively intact is Isabella's interview with her brother in prison. Indeed, in that scene even the notoriously incomprehensible 'prenzie Angelo' remains (3.1.94), which suggests that in the 1630s either it still made sense or its incomprehensibility was not a problem; in either case, we surely ought to stop trying to emend it. In all, the reviser cut 579 of the play's 2,660 lines, or about 22 per cent, a larger proportion than the *Macbeth* cuts, but still leaving a longer play. The cuts seem designed simply to reduce the length and complexity of the text, not to adapt it to any special conditions (a smaller cast, for example); one can almost hear the editor muttering 'More action and less talk'.

G. Blakemore Evans remarks of the *Measure for Measure* text that the cuts are for the most part designed simply to shorten the major roles.[6] Thus there is no attempt to reduce the number of characters or to alter sections that, in later revisions, were felt to be indecorous; and Evans observes that 'not infrequently, as one might expect, the heart has been cut out of some of the most poetically famous speeches in the play'. This is certainly true; but I would like to pause over the claim that it is 'as one might expect'. A great deal of what modern readers would call 'Shakespearean' has been deleted from these texts, what for us, and for three centuries before us, has made Shakespeare distinctive, remarkable, even recognizable. I do not think this is 'as one might expect', and it certainly contradicts vast areas of modern critical and textual assumptions about early attitudes toward Shakespeare and toward the integrity of his texts, at least after the publication of the folio. I want to consider some of its implications.

Clearly for this reviser, the Shakespeare text has no particular integrity. This does not mean that he does not care about Shakespeare; it means that by the 1630s (to put the date no earlier than we have hard evidence for), the concept of *Macbeth* or of *Measure for Measure* included broad areas of possibility and difference, and was not at all limited to the text of 'the true original copies'. What the reviser is producing are apparently not, moreover, conceived of as adaptations of Shakespeare. There were a number of adaptations of Shakespeare in the seventeenth century, but they represent themselves as new plays with new titles and new authors, not as versions of an original; as *Anthony and Cleopatra* became *All for Love*, *Measure for Measure* became *The Law Against Lovers*, *A Midsummer Night's Dream* became *The Fairy Queen*. In contrast, consider the title page of Sir William Davenant's *Macbeth*, which reads:

> Macbeth, a Tragedy: with all the Alterations, Amendments, Additions, and New Songs. As it is now acted at the Duke's Theatre.

No author's name is, or need be, supplied; it is clear that, for all the amendments, additions and new songs, the play is still thought to be *Macbeth*. Similarly, Dryden is unabashed to say, in the Preface to *The Tempest, or the Enchanted Island*, on which he collaborated with Davenant, that 'it was originally Shakespear's'. Since this text looks to a modern eye like a particularly radical case of revision—new characters and a good deal of new plot are supplied, and scarcely a third of the folio's dialogue is retained—one might logically take 'it was originally Shakespear's' to imply that it is his no longer. But this was the form in which the play held the stage as Shakespeare's *Tempest*, with only a brief interruption thanks to Garrick, until 1832. Similarly, Nahum Tate's notorious *King Lear* is advertised on its title page as 'Reviv'd with Alterations': not rewritten, but brought back to life.

These all suggest that the text of a play was thought of as distinctly, essentially, by nature, unfixed; always open to revision. This idea makes us very uncomfortable, and even critics who are willing to acknowledge the necessary instability of playhouse scripts in the Renaissance would probably want to argue that, at least after Shakespeare's death, the 'real' Shakespeare play was always what is preserved in the printed text, because all productions ultimately exist in reference to that. This makes perfectly good sense, but it makes sense only because of certain anachronistic assumptions we have about texts; and I am therefore arguing here first that it is not correct, and second that when the chips are down we do not really believe it at all.

It is clear, as we have observed, that for the professional reviser of the Padua folio, the Shakespearean text has no integrity. The fluidity of the written text, the divergence between published and performing texts, are historically authentic. And the claim of textual authenticity as a function of the author's hand, the folio's claim to preserve 'the true original copies' becomes an issue only when the plays are printed, and are then claimed to be authors' plays, not actors' plays. In fact, the degree to which the authority of a theatrical text is that of the author will be all but impossible to determine: what kind of true original can the folio text of *Macbeth* have been? In this case (and the case can hardly be unique) 'original' means that the copy is the one used by the company. The authentic text on which performances are based is the authorized text, which may well be a version of the author's original that has undergone considerable revision. Even authorial texts would have been far more fluid, far more unstable, than most of us, with our yearnings toward final and authoritative versions, will wish to allow. For us, texts develop and evolve toward publication, and publishing texts fixes them; we expend great efforts on 'establishing' texts that we can then call 'authentic'. The claim is historically inaccurate, and blinds us to the true nature of the works we are dealing with.

Indeed, it is not even correct to say that printed books in the period fix or preserve a text. Because of the practice of making proof corrections during the course of printing, and of assembling the finished book using both corrected and uncorrected sheets indiscriminately, every copy of the Shakespeare folio is different from every other copy. The same is true, to a greater or lesser degree, of all Renaissance books. To the literary historian the differences may appear insignificant, but to anyone interested in the history of the concept of the book and the nature of texts, the fact that such variability was not only acceptable but built into the system is of the essence. This does not mean that correctness was not an issue: early books include errata lists, and often urge readers to correct any other errors that they may find. As this implies, there was nothing final about the text in the book, even in books with errata lists.

Shakespeare's plays exhibit problems of vexed syntax, unorthodox spelling, and even at times seemingly nonsensical vocabulary. It is customary to blame these on the printer, but what if at least some were a feature of the text? That is, what if behind the obscure and imperfect text there is an obscure and imperfect text? Or, to press a little further, what if obscurity and incoherence are a feature of English Renaissance texts, but are not transhistorical categories, so that obscurity as a virtue of literary texts did not survive into the eighteenth century and beyond? It is clear that Shakespeare's age had a much higher tolerance for obscurantism than we have — at least, than we have in dealing with Shakespeare: we do not want Shakespeare to be George Chapman, and we certainly do not want to work as hard on Shakespeare as we work on James Joyce or Jacques Lacan. Perhaps the opaque passages in Shakespeare started out opaque, and that was part of the point. This certainly is clearly the case at crucial moments in *The Winter's Tale*; and when I proposed it in an article in *Shakespeare Quarterly* there were such howls of protest that I knew I must have hit a nerve.[7]

In one case, where I pointed out that 400 years of critical analysis had produced no consensus about a particular passage, an indignant colleague wrote me to say that the problem had been solved in an article published two years before. Doubtless it had been solved to the indignant correspondent's satisfaction, but that was no help to Pope, Theobald, Hanmer, Johnson, Steevens, Malone, and least of all to the readers of the first four folios. If nobody understood it until recently, that is certainly something we ought to take into account. It is very striking that the scribe of the Padua prompt-book and the editors of the folios do not emend the obscurities of their texts. Perhaps obscurity was not a problem.

Perhaps we ought to postulate an incomprehensibility topos in the period—we can certainly find support for this suggestion in Jonson and Chapman, and even in Spenser, who in his Letter to Ralegh characterizes the *Faerie Queene* as a 'dark conceit'. There are many problematic elements in the *Faerie Queene*: names get changed in mid-story, characters simply disappear, episodes never get concluded, Spenser himself even at one point confuses Guyon, the hero of Book 2, with The Red Cross Knight, the hero of Book 1; but nobody has ever blamed these on the compositor. This is just Spenser. Surely, in the same way, perhaps the obscurity in Shakespeare is just Shakespeare. Instead of modernizing Shakespeare, surely we should be treating it not as an inaccurate, ungrammatical, dysfunctional version of our own speech, but as a foreign language, and setting ourselves to learn the language and understand the assumptions of the culture. Shakespeare is difficult: can the texts really be sufficiently understood simply by adding explanatory glosses to the bottom of the page?

There are, in any case, no glosses in a theatrical performance. The original audiences must have missed a great deal, and modern audiences necessarily miss even more. But how do we know what the relation was between whatever texts have come down to us and what playgoers heard in Shakespeare's theatre? Since our claims about the effects of Shakespearean drama are based almost entirely on the surviving printed texts, it would seem essential to consider this question, and not simply to assume that we can read backward from the latter to the former. I do not, of course, pretend that we are in any position to supply an answer; but I also think that the question is a larger one than we have made it, and that it is necessary to understand its full implications before we try to move beyond it.

Consider a famous crux.[8] The account of Falstaff's death given by Mistress Quickly in *Henry V* 2.3 reads, in the folio text, '... His nose was as sharp as a pen, and a table of green fields....' This was the text from 1623 until 1733, when Lewis Theobald decided that Shakespeare's manuscript had been misread: that 'a table of green fields', which seems to make no sense, was incorrect, and that instead, in dying, Falstaff 'babbled of green fields'.[9] This emendation, indisputably a stroke of editorial genius, seemed to have restored what Shakespeare must actually have written. Bibliography here communicated with Shakespeare himself—or at least, with Shakespeare's manuscript before it reached the printer.

But if we agree that Theobald was correct, and that a compositor setting the type in the printing house was misreading Shakespeare's handwriting, what happened before the play got to the compositor? 'Table' is the 1623 folio's reading; so the folio's printer seems to be the culprit. But the only other substantive text, the 1600 quarto, in a passage that bears little resemblance to the folio text, at this point reads not 'babbled' but 'talk'—Mistress Quickly says she heard Falstaff 'talk of flowers'—and it is apparent that the folio was not set up from this very garbled quarto, but directly from Shakespeare's manuscript. So neither of our two primary sources reads 'babbled': 'babbled', even if it is impeccably correct, is all Theobald. What then does the quarto tell us about the folio's crux? Q seems to be a reported text provided by two actors; but if F's 'table' is a misreading resulting from a visual error in deciphering Shakespeare's handwriting, so would Q's 'talk' seem to be. In a reported text, however, the error ought to be an auditory one. If Q is really a reported text, then, the counter-argument would have to be that the reporters heard 'babbled' but remembered it as the simpler concept 'talk' (or 'talkd', as it is usually emended). This argument would be more persuasive if 'talkd' looked less like 'table'. So has Theobald been perhaps too ingenious? Is 'talkd' the source for both 'table' and 'babbled'?

Moreover, even if we agree that 'babbled' was what Shakespeare wrote, it might also be the case that Shakespeare's handwriting was hard for everyone to read, and was misread not only by the folio compositor but by the scribe who prepared the prompt-book, who would also have been working from Shakespeare's manuscript—and the prompt-book, after all, would have been the source of the actors' scripts too, and thereby of what the reporters heard, or misremembered.

Maybe the actors were (incorrectly) saying 'table' or 'talkd' all along. ('Babbled' seems to me an eighteenth-century rationalization, and a more likely emendation would be 'talked', as it is in the Folger Shakespeare text of the play.) For Theobald's purposes, however, what the actors said, what the reporters recalled, what all the audiences from 1599 to 1733 heard, was irrelevant; his communication was with Shakespeare's mind—or at least, with Shakespeare's bad handwriting. Theobald's intuition here effectively abolished both the performing and the textual traditions, the play's collective memory.

Surely the oddest thing about this sort of puzzle is to decide where the playwright fits into it. In 1599, Shakespeare was on the spot to see that the prompt-book and the actors got it right—how could 'table' (or 'talkd') be wrong? Didn't Shakespeare thunder '"babbled", not "table", idiots'; and why didn't the embarrassed prompter then immediately correct the error? How did the confusion survive the first rehearsal, to remain a permanent part of the play? And, of course, we do not know that they did: we really do not know what the relation was between what the actors performed and the manuscript that was given to the printer. The book is not the play. But emendations and revised readings have simply become the texts for us, just as Shakespeare is modernized to speak to us, not to a world long past. But Shakespeare's society was genuinely different from ours: magic and the supernatural were not merely poetic fantasies but facts of nature; the social hierarchy was everywhere apparent and violations of it had real consequences; religion was a serious and pervasive matter, and all too often a burning issue. We have edited all that out of Shakespeare.

In short, we face problems with all versions of Shakespeare, from good and bad quartos and the folio on down through the whole history of editorial and critical practice. And our appeal to the texts as the bottom line is far more problematic than, historically, we have been willing to allow, as becomes clear when we consider what texts we are appealing to. It hardly needs to be insisted that none of our texts is original, that every word we possess by Shakespeare has been through some editorial process. And even if a Shakespeare manuscript were discovered tomorrow, if we suddenly found those magical foul papers to whose elusive authority all editorial claims are ultimately referred, it would not simply declare its secrets to us. We would have to edit it before we could draw conclusions about it, and the editorial process would involve all the familiar decisions about what was really written, or intended, or meant, and these would inevitably be based on the editor's own assumptions about what the text ought to look like, and different editors would produce different texts. The conclusions, that is, really come first, not last; and whatever secrets Shakespeare's foul papers reveal to us will inevitably be perceived through the distorting glass of our own secrets. It is a mistake to believe that our sense of Shakespeare, whether we are scientific bibliographers or casual playgoers, is not 'contaminated', and indeed determined, by a myriad of other texts.

Indeed, Shakespeare's own working conditions, the requirements of his playhouse and the fact that his texts were to be spoken by actors, may be considered a form of contamination—as Humphrey Moseley says, the plays of Beaumont and Fletcher were 'mutilated' by performance. In any case, the fact that they are, and have always been so considered, can, I think, be demonstrated. Take, for example, the question of whether a particular passage is verse or prose. This is an issue that will be of much more significance to the editor and typographer than to the actor, who will speak the lines, however they are printed, as s/he sees fit. Here, from *The Tempest*, is a speech of Caliban's that appears in the folio as prose:

> I'prethee let me bring thee where Crabs grow; and I with my long nayles will digge thee pig-nuts; show thee a Jayes nest, and instruct thee how to snare the nimble Marmazet: I'le bring thee to clustring Philberts, and sometimes I'le get thee young Scamels from the Rocke: Wilt thou go with me?

Since Pope's edition in 1725, this has been construed as blank verse; and it does certainly have the rhythm of blank verse. But why do we treat it as verse rather than as prose that has the rhythm of verse? The assumption in dealing with Shakespeare is that verse is better than prose, and that since Shakespeare is the best poet, anything that can reasonably be construed as verse should be. Caliban has thus been dignified by the editorial tradition—he does, elsewhere, after all, have some of the most beautiful poetry in the play.

The conclusion of the storm scene at the play's opening includes an even more striking example that appears in the folio this way:

> *A confused noyse within.*
> Mercy on us.
> We split, we split, Farewell my wife, and children,
> Farewell brother: we split, we split, we split.

Can a confused noise be blank verse? Most editors have thought so. Pope not only believed that this was verse, but also that it must originally have been better verse, and emended the final line to 'Brother farewell: we split, we split, we split'. Capell was the first editor to perceive a difficulty, and printed the whole passage with the clauses separated by dashes—as confused noise, that is. This seemingly sensible decision, however, failed to persuade the vast majority of subsequent editors, who, almost without exception, have adhered to the folio lineation.

But clearly the question of poetry versus prose was a far less pressing one to Jacobean playwrights and to those contemporaries concerned with the transmission of their texts than it has been to the subsequent editorial tradition. It was, for purely practical reasons, of most immediate concern to the typographer. Many speeches could be either—verse lines in manuscripts generally do not begin with a capital letter. That was a typographical convention; and it is often difficult in manuscripts to tell whether a passage is intended to be verse or prose.[10] From the eighteenth century, however, the editorial convention has been to print everything as verse that could be construed in that way, the underlying assumption being that verse is better than prose. But for Shakespeare's age, no character was impugned who was detected speaking prose, nor was the dramatist's excellence vitiated if he was found to have written it.

The quarto and folio texts are our evidence for most of what we know about Shakespeare; but what are the texts evidence of? The editorial tradition has in fact allowed the texts to be evidence of very little. The agenda of editorial practice, at least from the time of Pope, has remained curiously unchanged: to deny differences and make Shakespeare as much like us as possible; and in this enterprise, ambiguities of sense and syntax have always been much more tolerable than ambiguities of form, of verse and prose. The former can be elucidated away or celebrated for their poetic complexity, but the latter undermine our whole sense of taxonomy. That this enterprise should be a constant, despite the radical shifts in taste over the past four centuries, says much for the continuity, indeed for the stubborn tenacity, of scholarly assumptions.

I conclude by considering the history of a small but significant emendation in *The Tempest* (1.2.374ff.). I am particularly interested here in what has constituted an explanation for the necessity of emending. There is a minuscule but perennially troublesome crux in the punctuation of Ariel's first song:

> Come unto these yellow sands,
>   and then take hands:
> Curtsied when you have, and kist
>   the wild waves whist:
> Foote it featly heere, and there, and sweete Sprights beare
>   the burthen.   Burthen dispersedly.
> Harke, harke, bough wough: the watch-Dogges barke,
>   Bough-wawgh.

Davenant and Dryden in their revision of the play, followed by Rowe in his 1709 edition, introduced a comma after 'kist', thereby making 'the wilde waves whist' a nominative absolute—the sense became 'when you have curtsied and kissed, the wild waves being silent', not 'when you have curtsied and kissed the wild waves into silence'. This reading was generally accepted throughout the eighteenth and nineteenth centuries, with a number of editors intensifying the absolute construction by enclosing 'the wild waves whist' between parentheses or dashes. No eighteenth-century editor saw any need to justify the emendation, and indeed few thought of it as a change at all. By the middle of the nineteenth century, however, the kiss began to require an explanation, and it was accounted for, first by Staunton and Halliwell, as a standard element of formal dances, which were said to have commenced with the taking of hands, curtsying and kissing. This assertion continues to be repeated in modern editions, though it has been revealed as a pure figment of the editorial imagination; kissing, as Alan Brissenden has shown, was not a customary part of the beginning of dances.[11] But the claim served to justify the comma: if the kiss is part of the dance, it is not the waves that are being saluted. A very few voices were raised in protest: Knight argued that 'this is one of the many instances of a poetical idea being utterly destroyed by false punctuation', and the old Cambridge editors were the first to draw support for the folio reading from the text itself, observing that Ferdinand's lines

> This Musicke crept by me upon the waters,
> Allaying both their fury, and my passion

indicate that the waves are acted upon in the way the original punctuation suggests.[12] Dover Wilson accepted the explanation of the kiss as part of the dance, but nevertheless let the passage stand without emendation, observing laconically, 'No stop in F'. Frank Kermode, in his 1954 Arden *Tempest*, was the first editor to question the dancing kiss. He followed the folio punctuation, but nevertheless felt a need to argue with it:

> To take hands and curtsy . . . were the first two steps in all dances, but the kiss normally came when the dance was finished [this too, according to Brissenden, is an error] . . . . Yet although this suggests that 'kiss'd' must govern 'waves', the notion is disagreeable, being grotesque in a context which does not require grotesquerie. The syntax should perhaps be allowed to be ambiguous.

The problem, however, is that as the passage stands in the folio, the syntax is not at all ambiguous. The only ambiguity in it has been editorial. Editors since Kermode, for the next thirty years or so, for the most part continued to opt for the comma, almost invariably without explanation. Northrop Frye's old Pelican, G. Blakemore Evans's Riverside, David Bevington's Scott Foresman texts all have it; while more recent editions such as Anne Barton's Penguin, Peter Holland's new Pelican, the new Folger, the Arden edited by Virginia and Alden Vaughan, and my own Oxford *Tempest*, which argues energetically against it, do not.

For this crux, Stanley Wells and Gary Taylor's 1986 Oxford Complete Works, and the Norton, which is based on it, go back not to the folio, but to the middle of the nineteenth century, and place 'the wild waves whist' between dashes, rendering it firmly parenthetical. The Oxford Textual Companion explains the matter this way:

> F would have to imply that the waves themselves are kissed into silence. This sense is not only excessively conceited; it is also practically incommunicable in a song. Kissing partners as a preliminary to a dance may be unconventional but it is quite plausible for imagined spirits.[13]

Kermode's complaint that the imagery is 'disagreeable' because it is 'grotesque' has been honed a little; the imagery is now 'excessively conceited', and this has become a reason to emend; but no attempt has been made to refer what are obviously matters of taste to any seventeenth-century standards. If we do undertake to do so, we will find it impossible to separate the grotesque and conceited from the elegant and classical in early modern sensibilities, as even a cursory look at contemporary iconologies (or paintings, or architecture, or even clothing) makes clear. Why Wells and Taylor find it 'plausible' for spirits of nature to kiss each other but not to kiss the waves is no doubt vain to enquire; but one person's excess is another's sufficiency. Long ago George Steevens noted a parallel in Milton's 'Nativity Ode':

> The winds with wonder whist
> Smoothly the waters kissed.

This is obviously an allusion to Ariel's song. Clearly the reader of 1629 admired what Kermode and Wells and Taylor three centuries later find so disagreeable— there is no accounting for tastes, but there is also no denying them. The 'Nativity Ode' is certainly conceited, to the modern eye excessively so, but that has never been invoked as a reason to emend it. As for the sense being 'practically incommunicable' in a song, this would depend on the setting (the original is lost), but it should be added that Shakespeare songs are not invariably models of communication:

> Hearke, hearke, the Larke at Heavens gate sings,
> And Phoebus gins arise,
> His steeds to water at those Springs
> On chalic'd Flowres that lyes:

Much critical energy has been expended on explaining the excessively conceited and syntactically baffling third and fourth lines of this song from *Cymbeline* (2.3.20–3), but no editor has suggested that their obscurity ought to be cured by rewriting them. In fact, in the surviving contemporary setting of the song by Robert Johnson, the puzzling lines are simply omitted. This is evidence, if we need it, that incommunicability is more likely to be a feature of the original text, or of the text in print, than of the play in performance.

In short, the instability of the texts, which the editorial tradition has consistently undertaken to control, is in fact what licenses editorial practice. Without recognizing that instability as evidence of anything at all, editors repeat precisely what they claim to guard against. The testimony of the text dissolves when contradicted by modern assumptions about verse and prose, by wholly anachronistic principles of taste and decorum, by notions of the disagreeable, the excessively conceited, the implausible, the incommunicable. As editors, we rewrite the plays we contemplate, and they become our own.

Notes

1. The Texts of Shakespeare

1 Tiffany Stern, *Documents of Performance in Early Modern England* (Cambridge: Cambridge University Press, 2009), 32.
2 See, e.g., G. E. Bentley, *The Jacobean and Caroline Stage*, vol. 3 (Oxford: Clarendon Press, 1956), 253–6.
3 Stern, *Documents*, 31.
4 Cyndia Susan Clegg, *Press Censorship in Elizabethan England* (Cambridge: Cambridge University Press, 1997), 5.
5 See Henry James and Greg Walker, 'The Politics of *Gorboduc*', *English Historical Review* 110, no. 435 (February 1995): 109–21.
6 Francis Beaumont and John Fletcher, *Comedies and Tragedies Written by Francis Beaumont and John Fletcher* (1647), fol. A4^v.
7 In the earliest version of the play in print, where the title is *The True Tragedie of Richard Duke of Yorke*, [etc.] (1595), the line appears on fol. B2v.
8 Tiffany Stern, 'Time for Shakespeare: Hourglasses, Sundials, Clocks, and Early Modern Theatre', *Journal of the British Academy* 3 (2015): 1–33.
9 Jason Scott-Warren, 'Milton's Shakespeare?' on the *Centre for Material Texts* website (https://www.english.cam.ac.uk/cmt/), entry of 9 September 2019.
10 Thomas Heywood, *The Rape of Lucrece* (1608), fol. A2^r.
11 Stern's detailed argument is in 'Sermons, Plays and Note-Takers: Hamlet Q1 as "Noted" Text', *Shakespeare Survey* 66 (2013): 1–23. See also the discussion of the transcription of plays by auditors (the examples are for the most part Spanish and French) by Roger Chartier, *Publishing Drama in Early Modern Europe* (The Panizzi Lectures, 1998, London: The British Library, 1999), 28–46.
12 Zachary Lesser and Peter Stallybrass, 'The First Literary *Hamlet* and the Commonplacing of Professional Plays', *Shakespeare Quarterly* 59, no. 4 (Winter, 2008): 371–420; Alan B. Farmer and Zachary Lesser, 'The Popularity of Playbooks Revisited', *Shakespeare Quarterly* 56, no. 1

(Spring, 2005): 6. Stern's response, with her different interpretation, is in the essay cited in note 11.

13 In fact, since the plays were on the same subject, they may have been thought of as the same literary property. See James J. Marino, 'William Shakespeare's *Sir John Oldcastle*', *Renaissance Drama* 30 (2001): 93–114.

14 The books were originally referred to as Pavier quartos, but recent research shows that Pavier was only minimally involved, and they should more properly be called Jaggard quartos. A measured, richly informative, but ultimately inconclusive account of the project is Zachary Lesser's *Ghosts, Holes, Rips and Scrapes: Shakespeare in 1619, Bibliography in the Longue Durée* (Philadelphia: University of Pennsylvania Press, in collaboration with the Folger Library, 2021). A clearer account is provided by Ben Higgins, *Shakespeare's Syndicate: The First Folio, Its Publishers, and the Early Modern Book Trade* (Oxford: Oxford University Press, 2022), 82–4.

15 A persistent claim has been made that a section of a collaborative play called *Sir Thomas More* written sometime in the 1590s is in Shakespeare's hand. Despite the fact that the play is included in the Oxford and Arden Shakespeares, the claim is very dubious: the play was written for a rival company, and the surviving samples of Shakespeare's handwriting, six signatures in four documents, provide too little evidence for comparison. For a summary of the arguments for and against Shakespeare's participation in the project, see Michael L. Hays, 'Shakespeare's Hand Unknown in "Sir Thomas More": Thompson, Dawson, and the Futility of the Paleographic Argument', *Shakespeare Quarterly* 67, no. 2 (2016): 180–203.

2. The Poems

1 The Lost Plays Database lists nineteen plays at least in part by Drayton, for which only the titles survive. The only play with which he was associated that was published was *The first part Of the true and honorable historie of Sir John Old-castle, the good* Lord Cobham (1600).

2 John Donne, *Letters to Severall Persons of Honour* (London: 1651), 103.

3 Sestiad 1.12–14.
4 By 1640, there were ten editions of *Hero and Leander*; sixteen of *Venus and Adonis*, and eight of *The Rape of Lucrece* (called on its title page until the sixth quarto of 1616 simply *Lucrece*). In the same period the most popular of the plays for readers were *Richard III* and *1 Henry IV*, each appearing in eight quarto editions. The most widely read of the other plays were *Richard II*, in six quarto editions, and *Romeo and Juliet*, in five.
5 M. W. A. Smith, 'The Authorship of "A Lover's Complaint": An Application of Statistical Stylometry to Poetry', *Computers and the Humanities* 18 (1984): 23–37.
6 See especially John Kerrigan's Introduction to the New Penguin *Sonnets and A Lover's Complaint* (London: Penguin Classics, 1986; rev. edn, 1995), 15–18.
7 Colin Burrow, 'Introduction', William Shakespeare, *The Complete Sonnets and Poems* (Oxford: Oxford University Press, 2002), 139.
8 Brian Vickers, 'A Rum "Do". The Likely Authorship of "A Lover's Complaint"', *Times Literary Supplement*, (5 December 2003), 13–15.
9 See Ward E. Y. Elliott and Robert J. Valenza, 'Glass Slippers and Seven-League Boots', *Shakespeare Quarterly* 48, no. 2 (summer 1997): 177–207, and the continuation of the debate in Ward E. Y. Elliott and Robert J. Valenza, 'So Many Hardballs, So Few over the Plate: Conclusions from Our "Debate" with Donald Foster', *Computers and the Humanities* 36, no. 4 (November, 2002): 455–60. A detailed version of the controversy is at https://www1.cmc.edu/pages/faculty/welliott/hardball.htm.
10 Burrow, *The Complete Sonnets and Poems*, 99–103.
11 Francis Meres, *Palladis Tamia* (London: printed by P. Short, for Cuthbert Burbie, 1598), Fol. Oo1v.
12 The title page to the first edition, published probably in 1599 but possibly as early as September 1598, does not survive, but the book was quickly reprinted, and a small number of complete copies of the second edition of 1599 are extant. The two volumes are ESTC S107201 and S106363.
13 It has been argued, most persuasively by Gary Taylor and Jeremy Maule, that two of the manuscript versions, late as they are, nevertheless preserve earlier readings than those of Thorpe's quarto. See Gary Taylor, 'Some Manuscripts of Shakespeare's Sonnets', *Bulletin of the John Rylands*

Library 68 (1985): 210–46, and the excellent summary by John Kerrigan in the New Penguin *Sonnets and A Lover's Complaint* (rev. edn 1995), 428, 441–53.

14 Robert Graves, 'A Study in Original Punctuation and Spelling', in *The Common Asphodel: Collected Essays on Poetry, 1922-1949* (London: Hamish Hamilton, 1949), 84–95; Randall McLeod, 'Information Upon Information', *Text* 5 (1991): 241–78. Stephen Booth and Helen Vendler in their editions of the Sonnets simply accept Malone's version as the poem; Colin Burrow acknowledges the problems but merely emends Malone's punctuation ('Introduction').

15 Both are cited by Burrow 'Introduction', pp. 103, 138.

3. Romeo and Juliet

1 I am indebted to Lukas Erne's edition of Q1: *The First Quarto of Romeo and Juliet* (Cambridge: Cambridge University Press, 2007). Also to Jonathan Goldberg's thrilling demolition of spurious bibliographical arguments in '"What? in a Names That Which We Call a Rose": The Desired Texts of *Romeo and Juliet*', in *Crisis in Editing: Texts of the English Renaissance*, ed. Randall McLeod (New York: AMS Press, 1994), 173–202. This chapter is adapted from my essay 'Two Household Friends: The Plausibility of *Romeo and Juliet* Q1' in my *The Invention of Shakespeare and Other Essays* (Philadelphia: University of Pennsylvania Press, 2022).

2 For Werstine, see 'A Century of "Bad" Shakespeare Quartos', *Shakespeare Quarterly* 50, no. 3 (Autumn, 1999): 310–33, esp. 326–7 and 332–3.

3 Erne, *First Quarto*, 24.

4 Bradin Cormack, 'Shakespeare's Narcissus, Sonnet's Echo', in *The Forms of Renaissance Thought*, ed. Leonard Barkan, Bradin Cormack and Sean Keilen (Houndsmills: Palgrave Macmillan, 2009), 130.

5 Quotations from the two quartos are transcriptions of the original texts, 1597 and 1599.

6 See Tiffany Stern's account of time-measurement in the period, 'Time for Shakespeare: Hourglasses, Sundials, Clocks, and Early Modern Theatre', *Journal of the British Academy* 3 (2015): 1–33.

7 The fifth quarto (1637) also reads 'he'.
8 Theobald undertook to explain the problem away: 'surely, it were easy to say, that no traveller returns to this world, as to his home, or abiding-place', but ignored the information about the afterlife imparted by the ghost, which Hamlet says we can never know, Lewis Theobald, *Shakespeare Restored; or, A Specimen of the Many Errors As Well Committed As Unamended by Mr. Pope, in His Late Edition of This Poet* (London: R. Francklin, 1726). Coleridge cited the note with approval, S. T. Coleridge *Literary Remains*, ed. H. N. Coleridge (London: Pickering, 1836), 2:227.
9 Samuel Pepys, *The Diary of Samuel Pepys*, ed. Robert Latham and William Matthews, vol. 3 (Berkeley: University of California Press, 1970), 39.
10 George C. Branam, 'The Genesis of David Garrick's Romeo and Juliet', *Shakespeare Quarterly* 35, no. 2 (Summer, 1984): 170–9.
11 [David Garrick, ed.], *Romeo and Juliet. By Shakespear. With alterations, and an additional scene: as it is performed at the Theatre-Royal in Drury-Lane* (London, 1750), sig. A3^r.
12 In my collection *The Invention of Shakespeare and Other Essays* (Philadelphia: University of Pennsylvania Press, 2022), 151–9.

4. Hamlet

1 A scribe, particularly one preparing writs for lawyers. The legal documents prepared by scriveners typically begin 'Noverint universi per praesentes . . .', equivalent to the English formula 'Know all men by these presents . . .', i.e., 'Let everyone be informed by this that . . .'.
2 In G. Gregory Smith, ed., *Elizabethan Critical Essays* (Oxford: Oxford University Press, 1904 and many reprints), 1.311–12.
3 *Wits Miserie, and the worlds madnesse* (1596), fol. H4v
4 Terri Bourus, *Young Shakespeare's Young Hamlet* (London: Palgrave Macmillan, 2014)—following, notably, Andrew Cairncross, *The Problem of Hamlet: A Solution* (London: Macmillan, 1936)—argues that the first quarto of *Hamlet* is the ur-*Hamlet*, a view shared by, among others, Harold Bloom, Hardin Craig, and Peter Alexander. See also Steven

Urkowitz, 'Back to Basics: Thinking about the *Hamlet* First Quarto', in *The* Hamlet *First Published*, ed. Thomas Clayton (Newark: University of Delaware Press, 1992), 257–91; Alessandro Serpieri, *Il Primo Amleto* (Venice: Marsilio, 1997).

5 Thomas Heywood, *The Rape of Lucrece* (1608), fol. A2ʳ.
6 Tiffany Stern, 'Sermons, Plays and Note-Takers: Hamlet Q1 as "Noted" Text', *Shakespeare Survey* 66 (2013): 1–23.
7 Fol. G2v.
8 Fol. G4v.
9 The note is a marginale in his copy of Speght's Chaucer (1598). There is, of course, no way of knowing precisely when Harvey wrote the memorandum. See the detailed discussion by Leo Kirschbaum, 'The Date of Shakespeare's "Hamlet"', *Studies in Philology* 34, no. 2 (April, 1937): 168–75. Harvey's volume is now in the British Library, Add. MS 42518. The note is on folio 422ᵛ.

5. King Lear

1 Kenneth Muir, 'Introduction 1. Text', in *King Lear*, ed. Kenneth Muir (Arden Shakespeare 2, London: Methuen, 1952), xv.
2 The best discussion, with a richly appreciative reading of Tate's play, is Richard Streier, 'Tate's Perceptive *Lear*', *Modern Philology* 121, no. 3 (2024): 326–51.
3 *The History of King Lear. Acted at the Duke's Theatre. Reviv'd with Alterations.* By N. Tate (London, 1681), fol. A2ᵛ.
4 Quotations are from the parallel texts of the Complete Pelican Shakespeare; line references are to this edition.
5 Steven Urkowitz, *Shakespeare's Revision of* King Lear (Princeton, NJ: Princeton University Press, 1980), focuses on a number of similar examples. See also Gary Taylor and Michael Warren, eds, *The Division of the Kingdoms* (Oxford: Oxford University Press, 1983); Sidney Thomas, 'Shakespeare's Supposed Revision of *King Lear*', *Shakespeare Quarterly* 35, no. 4 (1984): 506–11; Richard Knowles, 'Revision Awry in Folio *Lear* 3.1', *Shakespeare Quarterly* 46, no. 1 (Spring, 1995): 32–46.

6 Sig. G2^r. For this, and the following other examples, I am indebted to Richard Preiss, *Clowning and Authorship in Early Modern Theatre* (Cambridge: Cambridge University Press, 2015), 187: '*He playes and sings any odde toy*' (Robert Greene, *Orlando Furioso* (1594), sig. F4^v); '*Jockie is led to whipping over the stage, speaking some word, but of no importance*' (Thomas Heywood, *2 Edward IV* (1600), sig. L5^r); '*Enter Forester, seeing the other taken away; speak anything, and exit*'; (Anon., *Tryall of Chevalrie* (1605), sig. E4^r); '*Here they two talk and rail what they list*' (John Cooke, *Greenes Tu Quoque* (1614), sig. J1^r).

7 There are numerous problems with both the quarto and folio versions of the passage. In a speculative but highly persuasive essay that bears precisely on the transformation of script to book Richard Knowles suggests a plausible emendation of the folio passage, Knowles, 'Revision Awry'.

8 *The Plays of William Shakespeare*, ed. Johnson and Steevens, 15 vols (London: Longman et al., 1793), 14:302.

9 The records of the case were discovered and are discussed by G. W. Boddy, 'Players of Interludes in North Yorkshire in the Early Seventeenth Century', *North Yorkshire County Record Office Journal* 3 (1976): 95–130.

10 *The Plays of William Shakespeare*, ed. Samuel Johnson, 8 vols (London: J. and R. Tonson et al., 1765), 207.

11 Anon., 'On the Death of the famous Actor R. Burbadge', in *The Shakespeare Allusion Book*, ed. C. M. Ingleby et al., rev. edn (Oxford: Oxford University Press, 1932), 2 vols, 1:72

12 William Shakespeare, *The History of King Lear. Acted at the Duke's Theatre. Reviv'd with Alterations*. By N. Tate (London, 1689), 21. Subsequent page references are given in the text.

6. Pericles Prince of Tyre

1 *Ode to Himself* 'Come, leave the loathèd stage' (1629), lines 21–2.

2 *Supplement to the Edition of Shakespeare's Plays Published in 1778 by Samuel Johnson and George Steevens*, 2 vols (London: C. Bathhurst et al., 1780), 2:186

3 Stanley Wells, Gary Taylor, et al., *William Shakespeare: A Textual Companion* (Oxford: Oxford University Press, 1987), 556.
4 The Master of the Revels records a payment in July, 1613, to The King's Men for performing a play at court called *Cardenio*. Or at least, we think that was what the play was called: the record actually gives the title as 'Cardenna', and says nothing about it being by Shakespeare. The connection of this lost play with Shakespeare derives from a record made forty years later: the publisher Humphrey Moseley, who was undertaking to codify and publish the works of the major English playwrights, registered his intention to publish a play called 'The History of Cardennio, by Mr Fletcher, and Shakespeare'. Moseley never did publish the play; but it is surely relevant that he registered at the same time *The Merry Devil of Edmonton* by Shakespeare—this is a play that had been published anonymously in 1608 and in five editions thereafter, and had never been ascribed to Shakespeare. Mosely also registered two other 'Shakespeare' plays, *Henry the First* and *Henry the Second*, said to be collaborations with a minor playwright named Robert Davenport—Davenport was writing plays in the 1620s, well after Shakespeare's death. Moseley also did not publish those, and they have, like *Cardenio*, disappeared. Nine years later, in 1660, he registered three more plays by 'Shakespeare': *The History of King Stephen, Duke Humphrey, A Tragedy,* and *Iphis and Iantha, or a Marriage Without a Man, a Comedy*. Nothing more is known of them; and as for the ascription of any of these plays to Shakespeare, obviously no reliance can be placed on Moseley. But why have we been looking so assiduously for *Cardenio* and ignoring *Henry the First, King Stephen*, and all those others? The only answer probably is that for several centuries we have really wanted a connection between Shakespeare and Cervantes. In 1728 Lewis Theobald published a play called *The Double Falsehood*, based, he said, on a manuscript he had acquired of a Shakespeare play with a plot from *Don Quixote*—Theobald said he had three manuscripts of the play; he does not say the play was called *Cardenio*. The plot of *The Double Falsehood* is indeed adapted from the Cardenio episode in *Don Quixote*, but the character who should be named Cardenio, and who would therefore give the play its name, is named Julio. There is no evidence

beyond Theobald's word that the manuscripts existed—he offered to allow people to examine them, but did not in fact do so—and all three have disappeared.
5 *Pericles*, ed. Suzanne Gossett, Arden 3 (London: Arden, 2004), 16.
6 Lucy Munro, 'Young Shakespeare/Late Shakespeare: The Case of *Pericles*', *Actes des congrès de la Société française Shakespeare* [online] 34 (2016). URL: http://journals.openedition.org/shakespeare/3668 (accessed 12 June 2025).
7 George Wilkins, *The Miseries of Inforst Marriage* (London: George Vincent, 1607).

7. Macbeth

1 Stephen Orgel, 'Jonson and the Amazons', in Elizabeth D. Harvey and Katharine Eisaman Maus, ed. *Soliciting Interpretation* (Chicago: University of Chicago Press, 1990), 119–39. For the significance of witchcraft in the period especially in relation to King James, see Lawrence Normand and Gareth Roberts, *Witchcraft in Early Modern Scotland* (Exeter: University of Exeter Press, 2000), and the richly informative more general study by Laura Levine, *Afterlives of Endor* (Ithaca, NY: Cornell University Press, 2023).
2 Harry Berger, Jr., 'The Early Scenes of *Macbeth*: Preface to a New Interpretation', in *Making Trifles of Terrors: Redistributing Complicity in Shakespeare* (Stanford, CA: Stanford University Press, 1997), 70–97.
3 The book tabulates seven allusions, but in fact includes eight. *The Knight of the Burning Pestle* and a play called *The Puritan* refer pretty clearly to Banquo's ghost, and *The Two Maids of More-Clacke*, a parodic play by Robert Armin, the principal clown in Shakespeare's company, recalls Macbeth's 'Will all great Neptune's ocean wash this blood/ Clean from my hands?' Since Armin's play was published in 1609, this must be a recollection of *Macbeth* on the stage. Sir Thomas Browne in 1642 saying that he begins 'to be weary of the sun' is more likely a recollection of the printed text; Browne, *Religio Medici* (London, 1642).

4 For a fuller discussion of Pepys's response to the play, see my essay 'Shakespeare and the Kinds of Drama', in Orgel, *The Authentic Shakespeare* (New York: Routledge, 2002), 143–58.
5 Joseph Addison, *Spectator*, 45 (1711).
6 *The Dramatic Mirror*, quoted in Gamini Salgado, *Eyewitnesses of Shakespeare* (London: Sussex University Press, 1975), 299.
7 See Caroline Bicks, *Midwiving Subjects in Shakespeare's England* (London: Routledge, 2017).

8. The Shakespeare Folio

1 *Wits Recreations* (1640), no. 269, sig. G3^v.
2 For the acquisition, see W. D. McCray, *Annals of the Bodleian Library, Oxford, A.D. 1598-A.D. 1867* (London: Rivington, 1868), 66. The folio was one of a consignment of ten books bound for the library at the same time. Andrew Honey, the library's Senior Conservator, has recently determined that 'the First Folio was covered in a different more expensive high quality dark brown leather'. See Peter D. Matthews, 'Leather Cover of the Bodleian First Folio', available only online at https://www.academia.edu/30971029/Leather_Cover_of_the_Bodleian_First_Folio (accessed 12 June 2025).
3 £3,000 in 1910 was the equivalent of about $500,000 today—from a twenty-first-century perspective a modest sum for a first folio. The library had to make a public appeal for funds to keep the book in England; the purchaser thus pre-empted was Henry Clay Folger.
4 See William B. Todd, 'The Issues and States of the Second Folio and Milton's Epitaph on Shakespeare', *Studies in Bibliography* 5 (1952): 81–108.
5 Indeed, so problematic has the portrait seemed that it has been doubted that Droeshout the Younger can have been responsible for it, or even that he was an engraver. Mary Edmond, 'It Was for Gentle Shakespeare Cut', *Shakespeare Quarterly* 42, no. 3 (1991): 339–44, argues energetically that the folio engraver was in fact Droeshout's uncle, Martin Droeshout the elder; but since there is no surviving work by this artist with which to compare the Shakespeare portrait, the claim is speculative at best.

Edmond also claims that there is no documentary evidence for the younger Droeshout as an engraver, or indeed, at all after his birth record in 1601. Christian Schuckman, however, in 'The Engraver of the First Folio Portrait of William Shakespeare', *Print Quarterly* 8, no. 1 (1991): 40–3—obviously published too late for Edmond to take it into account—shows that the younger Droeshout emigrated to Spain in the late 1620s, and reproduces a number of engravings done by him there. One of these bears a striking similarity to the Shakespeare portrait, and leaves little doubt that Martin the younger is the folio's Droeshout. The explanation for his elusiveness is apparently simply that he was Catholic—perhaps a convert, since the family were Flemish Protestants—and found more patrons in Catholic Spain.

6 For the second issue of the third folio (1664) and the fourth folio (1685) the engraving was moved to its more normative position facing the title page, with the poem beneath it.

7 See above, note 4.

8 According to Eric Rasmussen, 'There are 53 known complete copies with all preliminary leaves and all 445 text leaves. An additional 19 copies are complete save for πA1, and a further 14 copies are complete save that they lack both πA1 *and* πA1+1.' (Private communication—thank you!)

9 The auction record for this book was set at Bonham's in 2020, when a hand-coloured copy sold for $437,813. A similar copy, however, sold at Christie's in 2022 for $60,480, and an uncoloured one sold at auction in 2024 for $65,885.

10 See Marjorie Garber, 'Shakespeare 451', *The Muses on Their Lunch Hour* (New York: Fordham University Press, 2017), 133–4.

11 Michael Dobson, 'Whatever you do, buy', *London Review of Books* 23, no. 22 (November, 2001). Available online at https://www.lrb.co.uk/the-paper/v23/n22/michael-dobson/whatever-you-do-buy (accessed 12 June 2025).

12 Ibid.

13 Ibid.

14 Edward Dowden, *Shakespeare* (London: Macmillan 1877), 55–6.

15 'No doubt some mouldy tale/ Like *Pericles*, and stale/ As the shrieve's crust, and nasty as his fish. . . .' *Ode to Himself* (on the failure of *The New*

Inn). Ben Jonson, *Poems*, ed. Ian Donaldson (London: Oxford University Press, 1975), 355. The shrieve is the sheriff, who collected leftover and frequently stale food for the poor.

16 For the Pavier-Jaggard quartos, see Chapter 1. Several were issued with false earlier dates on their title pages, to imply that they were not new editions. Two of the ten plays, *A Yorkshire Tragedy* and *Sir John Oldcastle*, were not by Shakespeare. As for the ghostly *Cardenio*, regularly cited now as a lost Shakespeare play, as I have indicated in Chapter 6 (note 4), I see no reason to assume Shakespeare had anything to do with it.

17 See the excellent paper on the early/late question by Lucy Munro: 'Young Shakespeare/Late Shakespeare: The Case of *Pericles*', *Actes des congrès de la Société française Shakespeare* [online] 34 (2016). URL: http://journals.openedition.org/shakespeare/3668 (accessed 12 June 2025).

18 For a fuller discussion of the genre issues, see my essay 'Shakespeare and the Kinds of Drama', in Stephen Orgel, *The Authentic Shakespeare* (New York: Routledge, 2002), 143–58; and my introduction to *The Tempest* in the Oxford Shakespeare (Oxford: Clarendon Press, 1987), 4–5.

Conclusion

1 Andrew Gurr, 'A New Theater Historicism', in *From Script to Stage in Early Modern England*, ed. Peter Holland and Stephen Orgel (Houndmills: Palgrave Macmillan, 2004), 71–2.

2 Francis Beaumont and John Fletcher, *Comedies and Tragedies Written by Francis Beaumont and John Fletcher* (1647), fol. A4^v.

3 G. Blakemore Evans, ed., *Shakespearean Prompt-Books of the Seventeenth Century*, Vol. I, *The Padua 'Macbeth'* (Charlottesville: University of Virginia Press, 1960); Vol. II, *The Padua 'Measure for Measure'* (1963); *The History of King Henry the Fourth as revised by Sir Edward Dering, Bart.*, ed. George Walton Williams and G. Blakemore Evans (Charlottesville: University of Virginia Press, 1974).

4 The beginning few lines of *The Winter's Tale* are also marked up. Facsimiles are in Evans, ed., *Shakespearean Prompt-Books*, cited above in note 3. The history of the volume is discussed by Lavinia Prosdocimi,

'Un fondo appartenuto alla *natio Anglica*. Il *First Folio* e altri libri inglesi della Biblioteca universitaria', in Ester Pietrobon, ed., *Intellettuali e Uomini di Corte* (Roma: Donzelli Editore, 2021), 205–16, which revises some of Evans's conclusions.

5   For a detailed discussion, including facsimiles of the edited pages, see my essay 'Acting Scripts, Performing Texts', in *The Authentic Shakespeare* (New York: Routledge, 2002).

6   G. Blakemore Evans, 'Introduction', Padua *Measure for Measure*, 1–2.

7   'The Poetics of Incomprehensibility', *Shakespeare Quarterly* 42, no. 4 (winter 1991): 431–7, reprinted in Stephen Orgel, *The Invention of Shakespeare and Other Essays* (Philadelphia: University of Pennsylvania Press, 2022).

8   For the complete argument and a number of other examples, see my essay 'Getting Things Wrong', in *The Invention of Shakespeare and Other Essays*, 83–98, from which the discussion of Theobald is adapted.

9   *Henry V*, 2.3.16–17. The emendation was first proposed in Lewis Theobald, *Shakespeare Restored; or, A Specimen of the Many Errors As Well Committed As Unamended by Mr. Pope, in His Late Edition of This Poet* (London: R. Francklin, 1726), 138, and subsequently included in Theobald's edition of the plays in 1733.

10 In Middleton's play *A Game at Chess*, which survives in multiple manuscripts, there are passages that appear as prose in some copies, verse in others. Some of the inconsistent examples appear in manuscripts in Middleton's own hand. See my Chapter 2 'The Example of *Gorboduc*', in *The Globe in Print: The Book of the Play in the Age of Shakespeare* (Oxford: Oxford University Press, 2024), 28–34.

11 See Alan Brissenden, *Shakespeare and the Dance* (Atlantic Highlands, NJ: Humanities Press, 1981), 97.

12 Both are cited in the Variorum *Tempest*; H. H. Furness, *A New Variorum Edition of Shakespeare: The Tempest* (Philadelphia: J. B. Lippencott, 1892).78.

13 Stanley Wells and Gary Taylor, *William Shakespeare: A Textual Companion* (Oxford, 1987), 614. The editing of this play (and the note) is by John Jowett.

Bibliography

Primary sources

Addison, Joseph, and Richard Steele. *The Spectator*, edited by Donald F. Bond. Oxford: Clarendon Press, 1965.

Armin, Robert. *The Two Maids of More-Clacke*. London, 1609.

Beaumont, Francis. *The Knight of the Burning Pestle*. London, 1613.

Beaumont, Francis, and John Fletcher. *Comedies and Tragedies Written by Francis Beaumont and John Fletcher*. London, 1647.

Browne, Thomas. *Religio Medici*. London, 1642.

Coleridge, S. T. *Literary Remains*, edited by H. N. Coleridge. London: Pickering, 1836.

Daniel, Samuel. *Delia and The Complaynt of Rosamond*. London, 1592.

Davenant, William. *Macbeth, A Tragedy*. London, 1673.

Donne, John. *Letters to Severall Persons of Honour*. London, 1651.

Furness, H. H. *A New Variorum Edition of Shakespeare: The Tempest*. Philadelphia: J. B. Lippencott, 1892.

Heywood, Thomas. *The Rape of Lucrece*. London, 1608.

Johnson, Samuel, ed. *The Plays of William Shakespeare*, 8 vols. London: J. and R. Tonson et al., 1765.

Johnson, Samuel, and George Steevens, eds. *The Plays of William Shakespeare*, 15 vols. London: Longman et al., 1793.

Jonson, Ben. *Poems*, edited by Ian Donaldson. London: Oxford University Press, 1975.

Lodge, Thomas. *Wits Miserie, and the worlds madnesse*. London: 1596.

Marlowe, Christopher. *Hero and Leander*. London: Edward Blount, 1598.

Marlowe, Christopher. *Hero and Leander*. London: Paul Linley, 1598.

Meres, Francis. *Palladis Tamia*. London: Printed by P. Short, for Cuthbert Burbie, 1598.

Middleton, Thomas. *The Puritan, or the Widow of Watling Street*. London, 1607.

Pepys, Samuel. *The Diary of Samuel Pepys*, edited by Robert Latham and William Matthews, 11 vols. Berkeley: University of California Press, 1970–83.

[Shakespeare, William.] *Romeo and Juliet*. London, 1597.

[Shakespeare, William.] *The First Quarto of Romeo and Juliet*, edited by Lukas Erne. Cambridge: Cambridge University Press, 2007.

[Shakespeare, William.] *The Passionate Pilgrim*. London, 1599.

[Shakespeare, William.] *The True Tragedie of Richard Duke of Yorke*. London, 1595.

Shakespeare, William. *Mr. William Shakespeares Comedies, Histories, and Tragedies*. London, 1623.

Shakespeare, William. *Mr. William Shakespeares Comedies, Histories, and Tragedies*. London, 1632.

Shakespeare, William. *Mr. William Shakespeares Comedies, Histories, and Tragedies*. London, 1663.

Shakespeare, William. *Mr. William Shakespeares Comedies, Histories, and Tragedies*. London, 1664.

Shakespeare, William. *Mr. William Shakespeares Comedies, Histories, and Tragedies*. London, 1685.

Shakespeare, William. *Pericles*, edited by Suzanne Gossett (Arden 3). London: Arden, 2004.

Shakespeare, William. *Poems: Written by Wil. Shake-speare. Gent*. London, 1640.

Shakespeare, William. *Romeo and Juliet*. London, 1599.

Shakespeare, William. *Romeo and Juliet. By Shakespear. With alterations, and an additional scene: as it is performed at the Theatre-Royal in Drury-Lane*, edited by David Garrick. London, 1750.

Shakespeare, William. *Romeo and Juliet* (The Oxford Shakespeare), edited by Jill Levenson. Oxford: Oxford University Press, 2000.

Shakespeare, William, *Shake-speares Sonnets*. London, 1609.

Shakespeare, William. *The History of King Lear. Acted at the Duke's Theatre. Reviv'd with Alterations*. By N. Tate. London, 1681.

Shakespeare, William. *The Rape of Lucrece*. London, 1594.

Shakespeare, William. *Venus and Adonis*. London, 1593.

Smith, G. Gregory, ed. *Elizabethan Critical Essays*. Oxford: Oxford University Press, 1904 (and many reprints).

Spenser, Edmund. *Amoretti and Epithalamion*. London, 1595.
Wilkins, George. *The Miseries of Inforst Marriage*. London: George Vincent, 1607.

Secondary sources

Allott, Robert. *Englands Parnassus: or the choycest flowers of our moderne poets*. London, 1600.
Bentley, G. E. *The Jacobean and Caroline Stage*, 7 vols. Oxford: The Clarendon Press, 1941–68.
Berger, Harry, Jr. 'The Early Scenes of *Macbeth*: Preface to a New Interpretation'. In *Making Trifles of Terrors: Redistributing Complicity in Shakespeare*, 70–97. Stanford, CA: Stanford University Press, 1997.
Bicks, Caroline. *Midwiving Subjects in Shakespeare's England*. London: Routledge, 2017.
Boddy, G. W. 'Players of Interludes in North Yorkshire in the Early Seventeenth Century'. *North Yorkshire County Record Office Journal* 3 (1976): 95–130.
Bourus, Terri. *Young Shakespeare's Young Hamlet*. London: Palgrave Macmillan, 2014.
Branam, George C. 'The Genesis of David Garrick's Romeo and Juliet'. *Shakespeare Quarterly* 35, no. 2 (Summer, 1984), 170–9.
Brissenden, Alan. *Shakespeare and the Dance*. Atlantic Highlands, NJ: Humanities Press, 1981.
Burrow, Colin. 'Introduction'. Shakespeare, *The Sonnets and A Lover's Complaint*. Oxford: Oxford University Press, 2002.
Cairncross, Andrew. *The Problem of Hamlet: A Solution*. London: Macmillan, 1936.
Chartier, Roger. *Publishing Drama in Early Modern Europe*. The Panizzi Lectures, 1998; London: The British Library, 1999.
Clegg, Cyndia Susan. *Press Censorship in Elizabethan England*. Cambridge: Cambridge University Press, 1997.
Cormack, Bradin. 'Shakespeare's Narcissus, Sonnet's Echo'. In *The Forms of Renaissance Thought*, edited by Leonard Barkan, Bradin Cormack and Sean Keilen, 127–49. Houndsmills: Palgrave Macmillan, 2009.

Dowden, Edward. *Shakespeare*. London: Macmillan 1877.

Edmond, Mary. 'It Was for Gentle Shakespeare Cut'. *Shakespeare Quarterly* 42, no. 3 (1991): 339–44.

Elliott, Ward E. Y., and Robert J. Valenza. 'Glass Slippers and Seven-League Boots'. *Shakespeare Quarterly* 48, no. 2 (summer 1997): 177–207.

Elliott, Ward E. Y., and Robert J. Valenza. 'So Many Hardballs, So Few over the Plate: Conclusions from Our "Debate" with Donald Foster'. *Computers and the Humanities* 36, no. 4 (November, 2002): 455–60.

Evans, G. Blakemore, ed. *Shakespearean Prompt-Books of the Seventeenth Century*, Vol. I, *The Padua* 'Macbeth'. Charlottesville: University of Virginia Press, 1960; Vol. II, *The Padua* 'Measure for Measure'. Charlottesville: University of Virginia Press, 1963.

Farmer, Alan B., and Zachary Lesser. 'The Popularity of Playbooks Revisited'. *Shakespeare Quarterly* 56, no. 1 (spring 2005): 1–32.

Garber, Marjorie. 'Shakespeare 451'. In *The Muses on Their Lunch Hour*, 127–54. New York: Fordham University Press, 2017.

Goldberg, Jonathan. '"What? in a Names That Which We Call a Rose", The Desired Texts of *Romeo and Juliet*'. In *Crisis in Editing: Texts of the English Renaissance*, edited by Randall McLeod, 173–202. New York: AMS Press, 1994.

Graves, Robert. 'A Study in Original Punctuation and Spelling'. In *The Common Asphodel: Collected Essays on Poetry, 1922-1949*, 84–95. London: Hamish Hamilton, 1949.

Gurr, Andrew. 'A New Theater Historicism'. In *From Script to Stage in Early Modern England*, edited by Peter Holland and Stephen Orgel. Houndmills: Palgrave Macmillan, 2004.

Hays, Michael L. 'Shakespeare's Hand Unknown in "Sir Thomas More": Thompson, Dawson, and the Futility of the Paleographic Argument'. *Shakespeare Quarterly* 67, no. 2 (2016): 180–203.

Higgins, Ben. *Shakespeare's Syndicate: The First Folio, Its Publishers, and the Early Modern Book Trade*. Oxford: Oxford University Press, 2022.

Holland, Peter, and Stephen Orgel, eds. *From Script to Stage in Early Modern England*. Houndmills: Palgrave/ Macmillan, 2004.

James, Henry, and Greg Walker. 'The Politics of *Gorboduc*'. *English Historical Review* 110, no. 435 (February 1995): 109–21.

Kastan, David. *Shakespeare and the Book*. Cambridge: Cambridge University Press, 2001.

Kathman, David. 'How Old Were Shakespeare's Boy Actors?'. *Shakespeare Survey* 58 (2005): 220–46.

Kerrigan, John. 'Introduction'. In William Shakespeare, *The Sonnets and A Lover's Complaint*. London: Penguin Classics, 1986; rev. edn, 1995.

Kirschbaum, Leo. 'The Date of Shakespeare's "Hamlet"'. *Studies in Philology* 34, no. 2 (April, 1937): 168–75.

Knowles, Richard. 'Revision Awry in Folio *Lear* 3.1'. *Shakespeare Quarterly* 46, no. 1 (spring, 1995): 32–46.

Lesser, Zachary. *Ghosts, Holes, Rips and Scrapes: Shakespeare in 1619, Bibliography in the Longue Durée*. Philadelphia: University of Pennsylvania Press, in collaboration with the Folger Library, 2021.

Lesser, Zachary, and Peter Stallybrass. 'The First Literary *Hamlet* and the Commonplacing of Professional Plays'. *Shakespeare Quarterly* 59, no. 4 (winter, 2008): 371–420.

Levine, Laura. *Afterlives of Endor*. Ithaca, NY: Cornell University Press, 2023.

Maguire, Laurie. *Shakespearean Suspect Texts: The 'Bad Quartos'*. Cambridge: Cambridge University Press, 1996.

Marino, James J. 'William Shakespeare's *Sir John Oldcastle*'. *Renaissance Drama* 30 (2001): 93–114.

McCray, W. D. *Annals of the Bodleian Library, Oxford, A.D. 1598-A.D. 1867*. London: Rivington, 1868.

McLeod, Randall. 'Information Upon Information'. *Text* 5 (1991): 241–78.

Muir, Kenneth. 'Introduction 1. Text'. In *King Lear*, edited by Kenneth Muir (Arden Shakespeare 2). London: Methuen, 1952.

Munro, Lucy. 'Young Shakespeare/Late Shakespeare: The Case of *Pericles*'. *Actes des congrès de la Société française Shakespeare* [online] 34 (2016). URL: http://journals.openedition.org/shakespeare/3668 (accessed 12 June 2025).

Normand, Lawrence and Gareth Roberts. *Witchcraft in Early Modern Scotland*. Exeter: University of Exeter Press, 2000.

Orgel, Stephen. *Imagining Shakespeare*. Houndmills: Palgrave/ Macmillan, 2003.

Orgel, Stephen. 'Introduction'. In *The Tempest* (The Oxford Shakespeare), 1–87. Oxford: Clarendon Press, 1987.

Orgel, Stephen. 'Jonson and the Amazons'. In *Soliciting Interpretation*, edited by Elizabeth D. Harvey and Katharine Eisaman Maus, 119–39. Chicago: University of Chicago Press, 1990.

Orgel, Stephen. *The Authentic Shakespeare*. New York: Routledge, 2002.

Orgel, Stephen. 'The Example of *Gorboduc*'. In *The Globe in Print: The Book of the Play in the Age of Shakespeare*, 17–38. Oxford: Oxford University Press, 2024.

Orgel, Stephen. *The Invention of Shakespeare and Other Essays*. Philadelphia: University of Pennsylvania Press, 2022.

Preiss, Richard. *Clowning and Authorship in Early Modern Theatre*. Cambridge: Cambridge University Press, 2015.

Prosdocimi, Lavinia. 'Un fondo appartenuto alla *natio Anglica*. Il *First Folio* e altri libri inglesi della Biblioteca universitaria'. In *Intellettuali e Uomini di Corte*, edited by Ester Pietrobon, 205–16. Roma: Donzelli Editore, 2021.

Salgado, Gamini. *Eyewitnesses of Shakespeare*. Lewes: Sussex University Press, 1975.

Schuckman, Christian. 'The Engraver of the First Folio Portrait of William Shakespeare'. *Print Quarterly* 8, no. 1 (1991): 40–3.

Scott-Warren, Jason. 'Milton's Shakespeare?'. *Centre for Material Texts*. Available from https://www.english.cam.ac.uk/cmt/, entry of 9 September 2019.

Serpieri, Alessandro. *Il Primo Amleto*. Venice: Marsilio, 1997.

Smith, Emma. *Shakespeare's First Folio: Four Centuries of an Iconic Book*. Oxford: Oxford University Press, 2016.

Smith, Emma. *The Making of Shakespeare's First Folio*. Oxford: Bodleian Library, 2016.

Smith, M. W. A. 'The Authorship of "A Lover's Complaint": An Application of Statistical Stylometry to Poetry'. *Computers and the Humanities* 18 (1984): 23–37.

Stern, Tiffany. *Documents of Performance in Early Modern England*. Cambridge: Cambridge University Press, 2009.

Stern, Tiffany. 'Sermons, Plays and Note-Takers: Hamlet Q1 as "Noted" Text'. *Shakespeare Survey* 66 (2013): 1–23.

Stern, Tiffany. 'Time for Shakespeare: Hourglasses, Sundials, Clocks, and Early Modern Theatre'. *Journal of the British Academy* 3 (2015): 1–33.

Streier, 'Richard. 'Tate's Perceptive *Lear*'. *Modern Philology* 121, no. 3 (2024): 326–51.

Taylor, Gary. 'Some Manuscripts of Shakespeare's Sonnets'. *Bulletin of the John Rylands Library* 68 (1985): 210–46.

Taylor, Gary, and Michael Warren, eds. *The Division of the Kingdoms*. Oxford: Oxford University Press, 1983.

Theobald, Lewis. *Shakespeare Restored; or, A Specimen of the Many Errors As Well Committed As Unamended by Mr. Pope, in His Late Edition of This Poet*. London: R. Francklin, 1726.

Thomas, Sidney. 'Shakespeare's Supposed Revision of *King Lear*'. *Shakespeare Quarterly* 35, no. 4 (1984): 506–11.

Todd, William B. 'The Issues and States of the Second Folio and Milton's Epitaph on Shakespeare'. *Studies in Bibliography* 5 (1952): 81–108.

Urkowitz, Steven. 'Back to Basics: Thinking about the *Hamlet* First Quarto'. In *The* Hamlet *First Published*, edited by Thomas Clayton. Newark: University of Delaware Press, 1992.

Urkowitz, Steven. *Shakespeare's Revision of King Lear*. Princeton, NJ: Princeton University Press, 1980.

Vickers, Brian. 'A Rum "Do". The Likely Authorship of "A Lover's Complaint"'. *Times Literary Supplement*, 5 December 2003, 13–15.

Wells, Stanley and Gary Taylor. *William Shakespeare: A Textual Companion*. Oxford: Oxford University Press, 1987.

Werstine, Paul. 'A Century of "Bad" Shakespeare Quartos'. *Shakespeare Quarterly* 50, no. 3 (Autumn, 1999): 310–33.

Williams, George Walton and G. Blakemore Evans, eds. *The History of King Henry the Fourth as revised by Sir Edward Dering, Bart*. Charlottesville: University of Virginia Press, 1974.

Index

Addison, Joseph 73, 109, 162
Aeschylus, *Oresteia* 129
Aesop 58
Age of consent 55
Alexander, Peter 157
Alleyn Edward 10
Allott, Robert 122–3; *England's Parnassus* 25
Anne of Denmark, Queen 68, 69
Apollonius of Tyre 97
Aristotle 40
Armin, Robert 77; *Two Maids of More-Clacke* 161
Auden, W. H. 35

Bandello, Mateo, *Novelle* 45
Barnes, Barnabe, *Devil's Charter* 101
Barry, Spranger 54
Barton, Anne 149
Beaumont, Francis 32; *Knight of the Burning Pestle* 161
Beaumont, Francis, and John Fletcher, *Comedies and Tragedies* 7, 131–2, 153, 164
Bellamy, George Anne 56
Bellini, Vincenzo, *I Capuleti ed i Montecchi* 45
Benson, John 32–33, 34
Bentley, G. E. 153
Berger, Harry, Jr. 106, 161
Betterton, Thomas 93, 96, 108, 109
Bevington, David 26, 149
Bicks, Caroline 162
Blackfriars Theatre 9
Bloom, Harold 157
Blount, Edward 94, 122
Boddy, G. W. 159
Bodleian Library 116, 162
Bodley, Sir Thomas 116
Boel, Cornelis 121

Booth, Stephen 156
Bourus, Terri 157
Branagh, Kenneth 70
Branam, George 54, 157
Brissenden, Alan 148, 165
British Library 124
Brooke, Arthur, *Romeus and Juliet* 41, 55
Browne, Sir Thomas 161
Browning, Robert 35
Burbage, Richard 85–6
Burghley, Lord (William Cecil) 18, 22
Burrow, Colin 22, 25, 27, 155, 156

Cairncross, Andrew 157
Cambridge University 59
Capell, Edward 146
Cardenna see *Cardenio*
Cardenio (lost play) 98, 160
Castellani, Renato 42
Censorship 4–5
Cervantes, Miguel de 160
Chapman, George 121, 141
Charles I 2
Chartier, Roger 153
Chaucer, Geoffrey 115
Chettle, Henry 7
Churchyard, Thomas 17
Cibber, Theophilus 54
Clapham, John, *Narcissus* 22
Clegg, Cyndia 5, 153
Closet Drama 6
Coleridge, Samuel Taylor 157
Collier, John Payne 128
Condell, Henry 9, 103
Cooke, John, *Greenes Tu Quoque* 159
Coppola, Francis Ford 66
Cormack, Bradin 156
Craig, Hardin 157

Crane, Ralph 120–1
Cumberbatch, Benedict 53, 56

Danes, Claire 56
Daniel, Samuel 17, 24; *Cleopatra* 6; folio 115
Davenant, Sir William 101; *Law Against Lovers* 133; *Macbeth* 108–110, 139; *Tempest* 139, 148
Davenport, Robert 160
Davies of Hereford, John 25
DelVecchio, Doreen 98
Dench, Judi 70
Dering, Sir Edward 124
Dobson, Michael 125–6, 163
Donne, John 17, 18, 34, 154
Dowden, Edward 126, 128, 163
Drayton, Michael 17, 25, 154; *Poly-Olbion* 121
Droeshout, Martin 121, 162–3
Dryden, John 34; *All For Love* 138; *Tempest* 139, 148
Duke Humphrey (lost play) 160

Edmond, Mary 162
Edward III (play) 128
Eliot, T. S. 35
Elizabeth I 18
Elliott, Ward E. Y. and Robert J. Valenza 155
Erne, Lukas 37–8, 42, 56, 156
Evans, G. Blakemore 133, 138, 149, 164, 165

Fairy Queen (*Midsummer Night's Dream*) 139
Farmer, Alan B. 153
Fletcher, John 26, 97, 160; *Tamer Tamed* 129—see Beaumont
Folger, Henry Clay 124, 162
Folger Shakespeare Library 124–125, 126
Folio 4, 115–26
Ford, John 26

Forman, Simon 107
Foxe, John, *Acts and Monuments* 81–82
Freeman, Arthur 27
Furness, H. H. 165
Frye, Northrop 149

Garber, Marjorie 163
Garnier, Robert 6
Garrick, David 54, 56, 109–10, 139, 157
Gascoigne, George 17
Geoffrey of Monmouth 73
Gibson, Mel 52, 70
Gielgud, John 42, 70
Globe Theatre 9
Goldberg, Jonathan 156
Goodyer, Sir Henry 18
Gossett, Suzanne 98, 161
Gosson, Henry 94
Gower, John 97, 115; *Confessio Amantis* 97
Graves, Robert 35, 156
Greenblatt, Stephen 26
Greene, Robert 7, 8; *Menaphon* 57; *Orlando Furioso* 159
Greene's Groatsworth of Wit 7
Gurr, Andrew 131, 164
Gutenberg Bible 123–124

Halliwell, James 148
Hammond, Anthony 98
Hands, Terry 99
Harington, Sir John, *Orlando Furioso* 133
Harvey, Gabriel 60, 158
Hayes, Michael L. 154
Heminges, John 9, 103
Henry VIII 115
Henslowe, Philip 57
Herbert, George 34
Herrick, Robert 32
Heywood, Jasper 58
Heywood, Thomas, *Apology for Actors* 5; *2 Edward IV* 159;

Rape of Lucrece 11, 58, 153, 158; *Woman Killed With Kindness* 12
Higgins, Ben 154
Hobson, John 133
Hoeniger, F. D. 98
Hole, William 121
Holinshed, Raphael 73, 112
Holland, Peter 149
Honey, Andrew 162
Howard, Leslie 56
Hughes, Willie 27
Huntington Library 124
Hussey, Olivia 52, 56

Iphis and Iantha (lost play) 160

Jackson, MacDonald 95
Jaggard, Isaac 123
Jaggard, William 12–13, 123, 127, 164; *Passionate Pilgrim* 29–30, 32
James I 68, 82, 86, 102–103, 107; *Basilicon Doron* 104; *Demonology* 104; *Works* 121
James, Thomas 116
Johnson, Robert 150
Johnson, Samuel 73, 80, 82, 84, 125, 159
—and George Steevens, *Plays of Shakespeare* 159
Jonson, Ben 7, 34, 58, 66, 93; folio 115–116, 121, 129, 141; *Alchemist* 7, 102; *Catiline* 6; *Devil Is an Ass* 102; *Masque of Queens* 101; *New Inn* 6, 93; *Ode to Himself* 159, 163–4; *Sejanus* 30; *Volpone* 7, 30
Joyce, James 141
Jowett, John 165

Keats, John 35
Kermode, Frank 148–9
Kerrigan, John 155, 156
King Leir (play) 73
King Stephen (lost play) 160

Kirschbaum, Leo 158
Knight, Charles 148
Knowles, Richard 158, 159
Kyd, Thomas 5, 58, 65; *Hieronimo* 66; *Spanish Tragedy* 66–8, 93

Lacan, Jacques 141
Langland, William 115
Lesser, Zachary 11–2, 153, 154
Levenson, Jill 51–52
Levine, Laura *Afterlives of Endor* 161
Ling, Nicholas 65
Lintot, Bernard 32, 33
Locrine (play) 127
Lodge, Thomas 57, 60
London 59
London Prodigal (play) 127
Luhrman, Baz 56
Lydgate, John 115
Lyly, John, *Woman in the Moon* 6

Malone, Edmond 33–35, 94, 95, 128, 159
Marino, James J. 154
Marlowe, Christopher 8, 17, 20–1; *Doctor Faustus* 93, 102; *Edward II* 6; *Hero and Leander* 18–19, 155; *Massacre at Paris* 6; *Tamburlaine* 5—and Thomas Nashe, *Dido Queen of Carthage* 6
Marshall, William 121
Marston, John 6; *Wonder of Women* 101
Marvell, Andrew 34
Master of the Revels 2
Matthews, Peter D. 162
Maule, Jeremy 155
McCray, W. D. 162
McLeod, Randall 35, 156
Meisei University 124
Meres, Francis, *Palladis Tamia* 28–9, 155
Merry Devil of Edmonton (play) 160

Index

Middleton, Thomas, *Game at Chess* 98, 127, 165; *The Puritan* 161; *The Witch* 101, 102, 107, 108; *Timon of Athens* 118
Miller, Arthur 2
Milton, John 10, 32, 34; *Nativity Ode* 150; *Samson Agonistes* 1
Mirror for Magistrates 73
Mitchell, Margaret, *Gone With the Wind* 66
Moseley, Humphrey 6–7, 131–2, 145, 160
Mostel, Zero 77
Mucedorus (play) 98
Muir, Kenneth 71, 158
Munro, Lucy 99, 161, 164

Nashe, Thomas 7, 57–8
New York Public Library 124
Newton, Thomas 58
Normand, Lawrence, and Gareth Roberts, *Witchcraft in Early Modern Scotland* 161
North, Thomas, Plutarch *Lives* 54
Norton, Thomas *see* Sackville
Nuremberg Chronicle 124, 125

Octavo 4
Olivier, Laurence 58
Otway, Thomas, *Caius Marius* 54
Overbury, Sir Thomas, *The Wife* 4
Oxford University 59

Padua, University of 52, 133
Pavier, Thomas 12–13, 127
Pavier Quartos 154, 164
Peele, George, *Alcazar* 10, *Orlando* 10
Pembroke, Countess of (Mary Sidney), *Antonie* 6
Pembroke, Earl of (William Herbert) 27
Pepys, Samuel 54, 108–9, 157, 162
Plague 3
Plautus 129
Playwright 2

Plot 1–2
Pope, Alexander 93, 127, 146, 147
Preiss, Richard 159
Preston, Thomas, *Cambises* 6
Prosdocimi, Lavinia 164–5

Quarto 4

Rasmussen, Eric 163
Romance 126–129
Rowe, Nicholas 31–2, 33, 127, 148
Royal Shakespeare Company 99

Sackville, Thomas, and Thomas Norton, *Gorboduc* 6
Salgado, Gamini 162
Scaliger, Julius Caesar 129
Schuckman, Christian 163
Schumer, Amy 77
Scofield, Paul 70
Scott-Warren, Jason 153
Seneca 57, 58, 59, 65
Serpieri, Alessandro 158
Shakespeare, William 2, 3, 8, 18–21; first folio 9, 42, 116–22, 123–4; second-fourth folio 13, 93, 96, 116 123, 163; *Antony and Cleopatra* 9, 94, 99, 128, 129–30; *As You Like It* 9, 99, 100, 104, 129; *Cardenio* 160, 164; *Comedy of Errors* 12, 103; *Coriolanus* 59, 87, 118; *Cymbeline* 76, 85, 119, 129, 15; *Hamlet* 3, 10, 11, 52–3, 57–70, 96, 103, 104, 105, 107, 108, 110–1, 113, 132, 133, 158; *Henry IV, Part 1* 93, 108, 133, 155; *Henry V* 9, 69, 84, 142–4; *1 Henry VI* 95, 98, 104, 127; *2 Henry VI* 3, 59, 95, 98, 104, 127; *3 Henry VI* 3, 8, 59; *Henry VIII* 26, 95, 119, 127; *Julius Caesar* 104, 118; *King John* 25, 95, 119; *King Lear* 5, 8–9, 10, 15, 31, 59, 71–91, 94, 96,

106–7, 110, 113, 119, 130, 158; *Lover's Complaint* 23–25, 26, 155; *Love's Labour's Lost* 3, 13, 30, 107, 123; *Macbeth* 9, 35, 52, 69, 76, 87, 98, 99, 101–13, 127, 133, 134–6, 140; *Measure for Measure* 52, 85, 127, 129, 133, 136–8; *Merchant of Venice* 3, 99, 129; *Merry Wives of Windsor* 25, 95; *Midsummer Night's Dream* 3, 104, 107; *Much Ado About Nothing* 129; *Othello* 12, 24, 59, 69, 108, 130; *Passionate Pilgrim* 29–30, 32; *Pericles* 5, 83, 85, 93–100, 126–128, 164; *Phoenix and the Turtle* 32, 76; *Richard II* 3, 155; *Richard III* 3, 59, 69, 93, 104, 108, 155; *Rape of Lucrece* 3, 16, 17, 22–23, 25, 27–28, 31, 155; *Romeo and Juliet* 9–10, 14–15, 37–56, 96, 108, 118, 155; Sonnets 26–35; *Taming of the Shrew* 3, 129; *Tempest* 12, 41, 59, 102, 104, 107, 109, 120–1, 129, 145–6, 147–50; *Timon of Athens* 118, 127; *Titus Andronicus* 3, 25–26, 84, 95; *Troilus and Cressida* 117–9, 123, 129; *Twelfth Night* 9; *Venus and Adonis* 3, 16, 17, 18, 21–2, 27–28, 31, 32, 60, 155; *Winter's Tale* 9, 76, 85, 87, 99, 128, 129, 141—and John Fletcher, *The Two Noble Kinsmen* 98, 127

Shakespeare Allusion Book 107–108, 159, 161
Shakespeare Quarterly 141
Shearer, Norma 56
Shirley, James, *The Gamester* 2
Shorthand 11
Siddons, Sarah 110
Sidney, Sir Philip 17–18, 31; *Arcadia* 73, 85, 99

Sir John Oldcastle (play), 12, 127, 128, 154, 164
Sir Thomas More (play) 154
Smith, M. W. A. 155
Sonnet 43, 44
Spanish armada 66
Southampton, Earl of (Henry Wriothesley) 3, 21–2, 27
Spenser, Edmund 17, 18, 24; *Faerie Queene* 73, 76, 142; *Letter to Ralegh* 141–142
Stallybrass, Peter 11, 153
Staunton, Howard 148
Steevens, George 35, 150
Stern, Tiffany 1, 10, 11, 12, 58, 153, 154, 156, 158
Strehler, Giorgio 81
Strier, Richard 158

Tate, Nahum, *History of King Lear* 73, 77, 83–6, 89–91, 139, 158, 159
Taylor, Gary 95, 149–50, 155–6, 160, 165
—and Michael Warren, *Division of the Kingdoms* 158
Terence 129
Theobald, Lewis 142–4, 157, 165; *Double Falsehood* 160–1
Thomas, Sidney 158
Thomas Lord Cromwell (play) 127
Thorpe, Thomas 24–6, 29, 30–1, 155
Todd, William B. 162
Tragicomedy 128–9
Tryall of Chevalrie (play) 77, 159
Turberville, George 17
Tusser, Thomas 17
Twine, Lawrence 97
Tyrwhitt, Thomas 27

Urkowitz, Steven 157–8

Van de Passe, Simon 121
Vaughan, Robert 121
Vaughan, Virginia and Alden 149

Vendler, Helen 156
Vickers, Brian 25, 155

Walsingham, Francis 18
Warner, William 25
Wells, Stanley 149–50, 160, 165
Werstine, Paul 37–8, 156
Whiting, Leonard 56
Wilde, Oscar 27
Wilkins, George 97–8, 99, 128;
    Miseries of Inforst Marriage 97, 161

Williams, Tennessee 2
Wilson, John Dover 148
Witch of Edmonton (play) 102
Wits Recreations (1640) 116, 162
Wordsworth, William 35

Yeats, William Butler 35
Yorkshire Tragedy (play) 95, 127, 164

Zeffirelli, Franco 52, 53–4, 56, 69–70